HIDDEN TEASURES
REVEALED

by

CAROL D. HOENER

Copyright © 2005 by Carol D. Hoener

Hidden Treasures
Revealed
by Carol D. Hoener

Printed in the United States of America

ISBN 1-597811-45-9

All rights reserved solely by the author. The author guarantees all contents are original and do not infringe upon the legal rights of any other person or work. No part of this book may be reproduced in any form without the permission of the author. The views expressed in this book are not necessarily those of the publisher.

Unless otherwise indicated, Bible quotations are taken from The Book software. Copyright © 1999 by The Learning Company and its subsidiaries and licensors, and The Holy Bible, New Living Translation. Copyright © 1996 by Tyndale Charitable Trust. All rights reserved.

www.xulonpress.com

FOREWORD

Nearly ten years when I first began hosting my daily afternoon radio program, one of the first dynamic couples I remember both calling in and meeting later in person were the Hoeners. Since then, I have gotten to know intimately both Jim and Carol as they have shared their testimonies, their heart and their soul with both me and our listeners many times.

Carol began to share her scriptural poetry with me and I would share it on air as it was not only inspiring but obviously a gift from God. When we did an in-depth study on a particular book, Carol's insight and personal revelation was just as effective in her journaling, as it was in both her prose and poetry. We all knew the Lord was calling her to write a book and share her testimony as well her writings to encourage and inspire others. She has now followed His lead and Treasures has been born.

As you read the unbelievable testimony of the trials and overcoming successes of Carol's life, you will both stand in awe and praise God for His faithfulness. Though many would have given up if they had faced these insurmountable obstacles of physical, mental, emotional, relational, and financial difficulties, it only taught Carol and Jim to rely more on the sovereignty of our Lord. You will be challenged to use this book as a catalyst to allow our God to work through the heartaches and roadblocks in your life just as Carol has beautifully surrendered her marriage, her family, her work and her gifts to Him.

In addition to her writings, her scriptural poetry will have you searching the depth of His Word as you relate the passages and the themes to your own life. As she shares personal "treasures" that often came during as well as after the testing you will see the obvious work of God's hand. Throughout the beautiful reflection on the names of God, intimate prayers and miracle after miracle, you will see demonstrated His infinite grace and mercy. Clear revelation has been given Carol and she shares her vision from the new Century onward, as well challenging you to see the calling upon your own life.

Through the personal insight as well as the variations in writings, you will both laugh and cry, but always be fully aware that every theme, every chapter, every word, is laid out before you to bring glory and honor to our Savior. Carol's life reflects this as well. I pray as I know Carol does, that you will both enjoy and be challenged by this book to grow in the Lord as you realize your own "Treasures."

By Dr. Debra Peppers

Dr. Debra Peppers is a retired English teacher, member of The National Teachers Hall of Fame, author and daily afternoon Christian radio talk show host of "Talk from the Heart" on KJSL in St. Louis.

TABLE OF CONTENTS

Foreword v

Hidden Treasures xi

CHAPTER 1 (A Glimpse of God's Glory)
    Testimony of my experience with God 13
    Poems
        God's Given Treasures......................................15
        The Treasure of Truth 17
        To Seek and Find Penuel 21

CHAPTER 2 (Gifts of God)
    Testimony of God's Hand on our life 23
    Poems
        To Receive from the Greatest Giving God.......39
        An Ode to be Saved..41
        Victory for Your Soul..43
        Welcome the Holy Spirit into Your Heart Today.........45
        The Gift of Grace..47

CHAPTER 3 (It's All About Him) 49
    Poems
        The Name You Can Trust..................................51
        Characteristics of Favor with God 53

Can You Hear Me?...57
In Jesus Name..61
A Forever Father..63
The Living Redeemer 65
A Sacrifice..67
God Be With You 69

CHAPTER 4 (Prayers for All People)
Testimony of Gods Blessing in Calamity....................71
   Dear Lord (a prayer for the unborn) 81
   Hear the Prayers (a prayer for the unborn)...........83
   Dear Mother of this child to be (a prayer for
      the unborn) 85
   Dear Lord (a prayer of hope for hurting people)..........87
   Dear Lord (A prayer for restoration for all people) 89
   A Prayer of Blessing for All 93

CHAPTER 5 (Blessings of Our King)
Testimony of a Financial Miracle 95
Poems
   A River of Praise 99
   The Final Revival 101
   What a Blessing it is..103
   Forgiveness..105
   The Honor to Live on..107
   An Offering in Stone...109

CHAPTER 6 (God in All Things)
Testimony of 9/11/01 111
Poems
   Why United We Stand 115
   Peace for Freedom...117
   9/11 Victory Prayer 119
   Believers Victory Song 121

CHAPTER 7 (A God for All Seasons)...............................123
   Welcome to a Place Called Heaven.....................125
   A Message of Hope and Understanding..............127

The Gift of Time 129
Year of Dedication and Declaration 131
Let Glory Reign in the Year of Your Holy One 133
The Year of Spiritual Eyes to See 135
The Perfect Gift for Christmas 137
Gifts from God for You..139
Thanksgiving Wish for You 141
An Easter to Remember 143
Agape, A Valentine from God 145
The Gift of Resurrection 147
Treasures of Fellowship 149

CHAPTER 8 (Treasures Revealed)
    Scriptures..151

HIDDEN TREASURES

I cherish your hidden treasures of **The Bible** that bless me every day.
and for every treasure I meet as I walk in your narrow way.
I thank you for the gift of **Psalm 23** to keep me free from fear and strife.
silver and gold cannot match the worth of the free gift of eternal light and life.
I thank you for the gift of **John 3:16**, the ultimate price for a sinner's plea.
only a spotless lamb and sinless life on a tree could cleanse me and set me free.
I treasure the gift of **John 14 verses 15-17** in that I will never walk alone.
for when I feel lost in this dark and dying world of sin He makes me feel at home.
I am grateful for the blessings of **Matthew 5:3-12** that gives me hope and joy.
As your promises are etched in my heart the world can never take or destroy.
I honor your gift of **Matthew 6:9-13** that you entrusted me to observe.
For only the highest glory, praise and honor are the least that you deserve.

I truly love the treasures of **Matthew 6:19-21** that you have entrusted to me.
With the priceless gift you have given me I dedicate it your highest glory.
I am awed by your love that you show in **Matthew 13:44 & 45** beyond measure.
Lord let me be the vessel you desire to be called your hidden treasure.
I am honored by the compassion of **Luke 15** that you would love me so.
I owe my life I gladly give to be washed and healed in your crimson flow.
I give myself as in **Romans 9:21 - 26** to be a crown from the miry clay.
Let my life shine your light so all who see your glory give you honor and praise.
In His Service For His Glory

By Carol D. Hoener

CHAPTER 1

A GLIMPSE OF GOD'S GLORY

The treasure map of this hidden treasure began in October of 1985 in what I thought was the end of my life but God had a different idea. I was 19 years old, just graduated from high school that year and I got bells palsy which caused my face to be paralyzed so I was feeling pretty down about myself. I had also made quite a mess of my life up to that point and I didn't want my mom and dad to waste any money on me to have the operation but they went ahead with it. All I wanted to do was die and get it over with so everyone could go on with their lives without me. I kept my composure up to the time I had my head shaved then I lost it and the doctor finally gave me an additional sedative. The next thing I remembered was opening my eyes and I been elevated out the room. I came to the front yard of my mom and dad's house and Jesus appeared before me. I knew it was Jesus because he was glowing nearly white but like a bright flame of fire.

He said, "Come with me I have something to show you." I can't tell you how it felt to be in the arms of Jesus except it was wonderful and what he showed me was even better. He showed me times in my life where he dispatched his angels to keep me from being killed, hurt, stabbed , shot or dead from a drug overdose. I had made a mess of my life and all the time I wanted God to forget about me. People were praying for me and God had his eye on me the and angels we protecting me from myself. I was really in such awe that

God would want me after all that. Then Jesus gave me a glimpse of heaven. It was perfection of beauty. Nothing lacking, nothing broken, a scene of perfect blend of color and texture and vitality. As quickly as I saw it I was in the Holy Place of the Lord and I was on my knees with my face buried in my hands because the Glory was so bright that I thought my eyes were being torched.

I said "Lord is this my time, do I get to live for eternity with you here in this beautiful heaven. Thank You, Lord I really thank you." Then God spoke and I thought I was going to combust. Hearing the voice of God was like feeling the rushing waters of coursing through my body. and He said, "No my child, I have something more planned for you in life. I have chosen you to give to others the Love that I have given you. You will reach millions of people with this love and you will touch their hearts with my love." Then I was back in the operating room. When I woke up I had the worst headache I could imagine. My mom and dad were there and they held my hand and told me to get some rest.

Everybody came to cheer me up and I think I ended up cheering them up. I couldn't understand why everyone was so upset. I didn't tell anyone at that time about the experience with Jesus because I was trying to figure out what God wanted me to do before I fell on my face. I survived the operation and didn't die and I am still a living example of God's love, He is not done with me yet. It didn't happen over night and it wasn't easy to travel but He has never failed me and he has been faithful to me from the beginning and will be there till the end and I give Him all glory forever for all He has done for me.

GOD'S GIVEN TREASURES

Jesus wanted us to know where the true gifts of God could be found.
The everlasting treasure of joy in our heart can only be heaven bound.
(Matthew 6:19)

Wisdom is a gift more priceless than treasure in the sea or sinking sand.
The secret is Godly fear for truth and forsaking evil brings understanding.
(Job 28:28)

Treasures of silver and gold bring destruction as proud men surely fall.
Great are rewards of humbled hearts as we exalt the Lord of all.
(Isaiah 2:11)

The treasured gift of freedom is paid with price no less great.
Only the Lord can lift the yoke of slavery and make our burdens light.
(Isaiah 10:27)

Greatest are treasures of Salvation and Righteousness given by
   God alone.
He only wants us to have the best and to bless us as we are his
   own.
(Isaiah 45:8)

Love for the Lord is the highest call endured with pain, and
   despair.
But the treasure of grace is sufficient when he gives us healing and
   joy in prayer.
(Isaiah 61:1-9)

Trusting in the Lord with hope and confidence yields much fruit of
   goodness.
As His treasures are created just for the purpose of making us truly
   blessed.
(Jeremiah 17:7-10)

Being the child of our heavenly king bring many treasure to spare.
But the value is even greater when in suffering we joyfully share.
(Romans 8:17)

This treasure isn't one which is found on earth or deserving of
   royal kings.
From sharing the priceless gift of life comes joy not matched by
   earthly things.
(Ephesians 3:8)

Faith may not find gold and silver in this home we now call earth
But we will be much greater reward in the treasures of spiritual
   birth.
Believe God, Receive God, Know God and Love God and you will
   have the treasures of God.

THE TREASURE OF TRUTH

A precious Jewel beyond the years of many kings and queens.
To the God of all, from the Saviors call, till we are the beauty seen.
From the potters hand we are made from the sin cursed sand.
To be transformed into vessels that carry the hope of a promised land.
(Isaiah 64:8)

Being freed from the guilt of imperfection and failure to be worthy within.
The priceless gift of gracious forgiveness was paid by Jesus, without sin.
(Hebrews 12:24)

With the faithfulness of the creator with the promise for us in giving.
How could we live our lives but through faith in our walk with the living.
(Revelation 22:11)

With the obedience as was given by Jesus to God, to give his body and blood.
What do we owe but the most faithful hearts to receive the bread and the cup.
(Luke 22:19)

Never to be alone in the promises God has made.
He brings his holy spirit to intercede for us each day.
(Romans 8:11)(Ephesians 1:13)

Once scarred in battle with the punishment of sin and death.
Now protected and powerful with the weapon of righteousness.
(2 Corinthians 6:7)(Ephesians 6:14)

Looking back on a time where freedom meant doing what pleased us.
Now able to look to the future where obedience to God is the vow we entrust.
(Exodus 19:5)

From a time where our minds were veiled with truth uneasily seen.
Jesus came to promise understanding when in his blood we believe.
(2 Corinthians 3:14)

When our lives were trapped by the laws that rule this world.
Jesus came to set us free with the fulfillment of Gods Holy Word.
(Matthew 5:17)

In times when the world seems to bring nothing but war and disease.
We can walk in confidence of the Good News which brings healing and peace.
(Ephesians 6:15)

Taking the wisdom of a world gone awry for people who have not faith.
We can take hold in the promise of hope through God's unfailing strength.
(Hebrews 6:18)

So now we can look at the sentence of the sin we would once pay.
And know that our road to freedom is just a humble prayer away.
(Romans 5:17-20)

We no longer have take the pain of hopelessness we once endured.
Our shield of faith will keep us protected with the promise we now adhere.
(Ephesians 6:16)

Everything that is new in us is greater because the blood sealed God's final promise to us
God gave the truest example of sacrifice for He knew for our sin, only His Son could suffice.
Out of all the Lord Our God has given to show his love for us.
Let us look at the book that sealed the promise and give back the love within us.
(Hebrews 9)

In unending gratitude to God for his everlasting covenant.

TO SEEK AND FIND PENUEL

There really is no where to find
The beauty can be seen by even the blind.
For everywhere in the world you see
Our Heavenly Father made for you and me.
When it is healing in our body we long to feel.
It's as close as a friend when we join to kneel.
When in he midst of war we find need for peace.
Our harmony with others God blesses so sweet.
When we are lost and it is God's will we seek.
We can ask in confidence that He hears us speak.
When life gets hard and times of trouble come.
Our greatest courage comes from our Holy One.
When our lives seem small and we feel left out.
Just sharing our faith with others brings joy about.
When we feel an empty yearning for hidden desires inside.
God seeks us out and finds us from his love we cannot hide.
We don't have to struggle to seek his face.
Camp Penuel is here to help finish the race.

To find the treasure of Penuel look at:
Jeremiah 23:34 (God's Beauty)
James 5:16 (healing)
Psalm 133:1-3 (peace)
1 John 5:14 (confidence)

John 14:27 (courage)
Philippians 1:25 (joy)
Jeremiah 29:13 (desires of the heart)

This poem was inspired by Harry Duma the founder of Camp Penuel a place that offers inner city kids a chance to go to camp and teaches them about finding Jesus in their own lives.

CHAPTER 2

GIFTS OF GOD

The easiest way of finding hidden treasures of God is to see the handiwork in the lives he has touched. Our lives are a living treasure to show the goodness and mercy of God. In 17 years God has brought my husband Jim and myself from living in a car and struggling to find money for food and other things to having a home and a ministry and writing the treasure map so that others will see the awesomeness of God. The following is just a glimpse of what God can do for anyone that want's to find his hidden treasure.

Two years after my brain surgery my hair had grown back and I started working about 6 months later. I got enough money saved up to put a down payment on a car and had the rug pulled out from under me when the company I worked for went out of business. A few months later on Christmas I found myself missing my brother and wanting to go for a drive. I was doing okay until the car slid on some loose gravel and spun around and uprooted a tree and I was stuck. I was there for a half hour and nobody came so I decided to walk to a phone since there were no cell phones at the time.

Miracles number three and four were knocking on my door. As I was walking down the road I saw 2 pit bulls coming for me top speed. The only thing I could think of was to jump into a tree. I jumped about 4 feet straight up into the tree but I could feel the hot breath of the pit bulls snapping their jaws at my feet and then their owner called for them and they went away. I was safe or so I thought. I got down out of the tree and started walking and along came 3 Dobermans. They were running loose and found me and started running after me. I started running as fast as I could up a hill and I thought I was not going to be able to make it and the owner of the dogs called them and they lost interest in me and I was safe yet another for a moment. I leaned against a tree for a moment to catch my breath and made it to a phone to call my dad. The car took more punishment than I did. I got a break because I knew someone who did repairs on cars and got the job done at a fraction of the cost.

I was without a car until I got it fixed. My mom and dad didn't want me to wreck another car again so they decided to take me back and forth to work. Miracle number five was literally just around the corner. My mom dropped me off at a temporary job and I found myself nearly getting killed by a lady named Kong who didn't like me because I didn't understand her so I got my timecard signed and got out of yet another life threatening situation and was in pursuit of a telephone again. To my relief there was a Denny's not too far away. I made it to Denny's and sat down and ordered my heartburn special and went to make a call to my mom.

On my way to the phone I caught a glimpse of this really cute guy sitting at the counter and he smiled at me but I didn't think much about it. My mom said it would be a while before she could come so I sat down and drank about three cups of coffee and ate my chili with onions and cheese and french fries. Then I looked up and this cute guy was standing at my table and he asked if anyone was sitting across from and asked if he could join me. The really cute guy was future husband Jim. We started talking and we before I knew it my mom came driving up and he asked me for my phone number. I found a napkin and a pen and wrote my phone number down. I didn't think he would call me back but he did and we have been together ever since.

Our love story is one of overcoming some great obstacles but even greater victories but we were destined to be together and will be for eternity. Three days after we met was Valentines Day. He brought me two roses. One for me and one for my mom and nobody ever did that for me before. That night I had a dream that I had dreamed when I was 8 years old which was about a tall and handsome man riding a blue motorcycle and wearing a black leather jacket and Jim came a couple days later in the same way and I realized that Jim was going to be the man I was going to marry. The problem was that nobody else agreed due to some technicalities. I later found out that Jim was married but in the middle of a divorce which would be finalized in May and the fact that he was 36 years old at the time while I was just turning 21 didn't make us popular either.

I got my car taken from me because I couldn't make the payments so it went to my sister so she could get back and forth to college. My beginnings with Jim's mom and dad did not go so well either but nothing could keep us apart. When Jim was getting ready to sign his divorce papers and get everything finalized everyone caught on to the idea that were going to try to be married. A few days prior we got our birth certificates and Jim went to the court house to get our marriage license. My parents arranged for me to stay with their friends in Grey Summit and if I hadn't told Jim about them before I left he never would have been able to find me. Jim got his divorce final and he got a stipulation payment from his ex-wife since she got to keep the house. She had to give him 800.00 and had to pay him 100.00 a month for 2 years after that.

Jim got a Volkswagen Bus and got it fixed and running and he was in pursuit of retrieving his new bride and after three hours of camping out on my mom and dad's front porch my sister gave him the number where I could be reached. Jim got a hold of me and gave me the ultimatum. I asked them how to get to their house so he could get me and they said they were given order to shoot him if he came around so he gave me a half hour to meet him at the top of the hill or I would never see him again. I literally had to walk a mile up hill and then I got chased by wild dogs but I made it and Jim was not to be found. I started walking down the road and I heard a funny noise and I turned around and I saw Jim and the Volkswagen Bus that we lived in for the next 6 months. We were constantly struggling to find places where we could park and camp out in the midst of trying to keep the car running.

Most relationships would have ended before having to live in a Volkswagen but who God joined together no man could separate. We didn't officially get married until August 20 1987 because according to the divorce stipulation Jim couldn't get married for 3 months or his ex-wife wouldn't have to pay him the money. During that summer of living in the Volkswagen Bus we did manage to have good times. We were even happy to be together and thanks to our Clarabell (the Volkswagen) we got to meet our best friends that are still our best friends today. We had just gotten the starter fixed on Clarabell and we were at Denny's planning out the days events and we were getting ready to go to someone's house and we ran across a couple who were looking for a ride. John and Barb lived out in Robertsville and they had already walked from the arch to where we picked them up and we took them to their house and we stayed out there a lot. Barb introduced us to the agape house to help us with food and they introduced us to some other friends. John and Barb were really a blessing to us and have been for 17 years.

Later on that year Jim had dropped me off at my mom and dads house because we couldn't continue living in the bus. We had just paid someone to put a fuel pump in and it had a real strong gas smell and we couldn't figure out why then Jim stopped in a gas station and Clarabell was on fire and spitting sulfur. It took three fire trucks to get the fire out but Clarabell did not recover. Three months later Jim's dad bought Jim a new truck so he could get back and forth to work. Even though we could not live together we saw each other every night. A few weeks after Jim got his truck he was stopping by his mom and dads house and found some mail that came for him. There were a couple of checks for a couple thousand dollars. They were not really intended for Jim but for his dad to cover the cost of the car but Jim got the checks and cashed them and we were together again. At first we lived in a motel and then the money ran out then Jim had to have an operation on his hernia so we were having to live apart again.

We spent nearly a year living like that and the following Christmas Jim decided he would rather have me than his truck so we took the truck to a car dealership and traded it in on a less expensive car and we got 2 thousand dollars. This time when we got the money we found an apartment that was ready to move into for 200 dollars a month and we moved in December 31, 1988 and we never lived apart since then. We were definitely not in good graces after we sold the truck that his dad bought for us and for two years I was not allowed near their house so every Sunday night Jim dropped me off at Denny's will he sat and had dinner with his folks.

In 1989 I started collecting unemployment and found out about a school that was accepting new students to enroll in their classes. I decided I didn't have anything to lose and I wouldn't have to pay anything until the school was over so I checked it out. I found out that I had potential that I never knew before. Jim and I both decided it would be a good idea so I started their Computer Operations classes in February. I did excellent, I made honor roll every month and excelled in everything a learned. I got a job at the end of the 7 months through their job placement and Jim's mom and dad decided I was not so bad after we invited them to my graduation and they found out that I graduated in the top 5 of my class. For the first time in my life everyone was proud of me and I was actually proud of myself. I felt there was finally hope for me to make something good out of my life.

During our first couple of years together, I believe the biggest key to our success was our relationship with the Lord. We started going to the Presbyterian Church where Jim went most of his life. I had no idea what to expect because I started out going to Pentecostal church and then went to a Baptist church during my teenage years. I was never forced to go to church by my parents and I went to church because I enjoyed it. Even though our religious upbringing was different we both had a mutual love for God and Jesus and He was very important to both of us in both of our lives and especially in our marriage. During the time when we first started living in that apartment we started watching Robert Schuller on the "Hour of Power". Even though we were not going to church we were growing in the Lord and getting fed spiritually and we continued to be blessed more and more.

After 3 years of being together we were finally accepted as husband and wife and everyone realized we were not going to leave each other. Jim and I started working off the money that we owed his dad for the truck which consisted of mowing the lawn and washing cars and windows and washing laundry and having family dinner every Sunday Night. My family was beginning to accept Jim as well. My sister asked me to be a brides maid in her wedding and she invited Jim and His parents to the wedding. I was working at a book publishing company where my sister worked and we saw each other every day. Jim would drop me off and my sister would give me a ride to work and Jim would pick me up. My sister's wedding was a real big day for everybody. Jim's mom and dad went to the reception after the wedding and met my brother and sat down with our folks and then they asked us if would be able to take vacation the following year and asked if we could go to Bermuda with them to Celebrate their 50th wedding anniversary. We excitedly accepted the invitation.

A year later we were given another miracle. Two weeks before Jim and I were going to be in Bermuda I had the scare of my life. I was working 2 jobs and my second job was a second shift job so Jim had dinner with his folks a lot since I was gone most of the time. Jim had been working on his motorcycle a lot one day and he came to see me at lunch. He was so happy that he saved all that money but he was tired because it took him all day to do it. When I got off work that night I was on my way home and I noticed a motorcycle on the side of the highway but I didn't think it was Jim's. So I just drove on home and when I got home Jim was not there. By now I was a little upset because there was no reason for him not to be home and then I remembered the motorcycle on the side of the road and began to panic. I didn't know what to do except wait and hopefully I would get a call from him or he would just show up. I got a phone call and it was Jim. He said "Hello, this is your friendly neighborhood motorcycle man and I am here at St. Louis University Hospital and I am okay I just need you to pick me up."

Jim told me how he was on his way home and he got behind a car and he could barely see it because the guy's tail lights were so dim. He looked down at his speedometer and the next thing he knew he was flying over the handle bars and he landed on the hood of the guys car and then landed on the ground. He said all he could remember at that time was saying Okay Lord, here I come, I am ready. He thought his time was up. They took him by ambulance to the hospital and he just walked away from the accident with a sprain and a big bump on his hip. He was afraid he would not be able to go to Bermuda but he healed quickly and we were on our way to Bermuda where we spent our 4 year anniversary.

Our lives were changing for the better by leaps and bounds after Bermuda. Although we still had our share of bumps and bruises we were conquering all our mountains and overcoming setbacks. Every time something bad would happen to us, God showed his incredible love and mercy and we ended up in better shape than we were before. We never had to go hungry and we never had to worry about having a place to live. A couple months after we got back from Bermuda we were living in a small 2 room apartment that didn't even have a bathtub and the kitchen consisted of a kitchen sink on one side to dishes and a stove at the other end of it to cook. We had our refrigerator in the living room area and we had no place for a couch and when we first moved into the place it was like "Green Acres" because we kept having to buy fuses. One night we left a candle burning and we were so tired we forgot about till I woke up and started choking and Jim woke up and found the VCR and TV on fire, the next thing I knew Jim was throwing the VCR out the door and we got the fire out but Jim burned his hand and the smell was beyond livable so we called his dad and stayed at their house that night. It was a miracle that we did not get burned up in that fire. It was also a miracle that the VCR and the TV survived the fire. The guy I was working for at the time was real nice and understanding and he really helped us out a lot. One time be bought a case of macaroni and cheese for us to supplement our meals when we were struggling financially. Unfortunately that job ended the day before Thanksgiving but I was really blessed and got to be a blessing for others.

In March of the following year our lease was up and we were having to find another place to live and God miraculously made an apartment available in Jim's dad's apartment building. Not only did we get to move into a nicer bigger apartment but we got to stay there for free. We stayed in that apartment rent free for 7 years. We even got to get our very first puppy that we had wanted since we were married and had to give up my 21st birthday dog. We did get to have a cat in our first apartment but we had to give her up when we moved into the smaller one. Katy was born on presidents day in

1992. We looked in the news paper for a long time because we wanted to give a good home to a dog that needed one. We knew we were going to have to pay money to get the shots and everything so it made sense that we would look for a free one.

We found an ad for free German Shepherd puppies and we found the place and the mother of the puppies was an all white German Shepherd and they did not know what the father was. We were there for almost a half hour and we were surrounded by playful energetic puppies but we couldn't take our eye of a little puppy in the corner taking a nap. Jim held her for a few minutes and decided Katy was the one for us. Katy was the runt of the litter but she was the one we wanted so we took her home that day and she is still acts like a puppy to this day. We had originally called her Lady since she was born on presidents day and since she was our first she was the first lady. We named her Katy after we got her fixed and she could no longer be a lady.

A few months after I got laid off from the one job Jim and I found a temporary job together and we got to really make a lot of money because we got a lot of overtime. We worked 7 days a week and about 10 hours a day. It really wore us out but the money was great and we got to get caught up on our bills and since we didn't have to pay rent we really had a lot of money to spare. It was during this time that we started to tithe like we never tithed before. We became Eagle Club Members of the Crystal Cathedral which we were for the whole 7 years we lived rent free. Unfortunately we had learned to "Discover" and during the time we should have been paying off bills we were accumulating them through credit card debt.

I finally got a good full time job with insurance benefits and full time pay and I was making more than minimum wage. The only problem was I worked for the most evil person I had ever met. At first he didn't seem to be a problem and everyone else seemed pretty cool but the manager brought me to tears a number of times. Things really got heated up while I was working on his full length catalog and we both realized I could never make him happy. A year and a half after I worked in the office his sister decided she didn't like me either so they gave me a dollar an hour raised and moved me out to the warehouse to do industrial work and they were happy and I got my sanity back for a little while. I got to work with the managers son when I worked in the warehouse and got to take him in when his mother kicked him out until his dad found out and that put more stress on our already heated relationship. Later on that year I got diagnosed with carpal tunnel and had to have surgery. I escaped from his wrath the following spring when I started working for a Chiropractic Clinic.

Working for the Chiropractic Clinic was the best thing that had ever happened to me up to that point. I got to meet people every day and help them and encourage them. I also worked for a wonderful Chiropractor who was inspiring and thoughtful and taught me a lot about health and nutrition. That job was not without it's drawback as well. The manager of the Clinic was never a happy person about anything and he was not afraid to show it. I got to meet a lot of neat people when I worked there. I met a superintendent of a school and the owner of a restaurant and I met the owner of a motorcycle shop. The guy who owned the motorcycle shop found a Doberman and took it in and took care of it and found out that the dog was ready to deliver puppies. They had already cropped the dogs tails and got them wormed and they were just giving them away because they couldn't handle having 7 Dobermans. That is how we got Happy Golucky who is the most loyal and devoted dog we ever had.

Two weeks before Christmas that year in 1996, the manager laid me off because there was not enough business to pay me to work there so I was without a job and a few days after that I got real sick and had to stay in the hospital for 8 days. I would have let it get the worst of me but I my roommate in the hospital was the mother of a praise and worship singer at the church we had been attending. We couldn't believe we were talking about the same person and then when I mentioned that her name was Jacque Deshetler I found out that my room mate was Jacque's mom. We really got along well and we stayed in touch after we got out of the hospital. We even saw each other Christmas Eve Night when they had the special music service. That was just another way God used something that the Devil meant to use against us and turned it around for good.

A few months later I was faced with having a hysterectomy. During the time I faced conflict on every side of the issue. I had the doctors telling me that I would just continue having the problem that made me go into the hospital and having the surgery would guarantee I would not have the same problem again. Then I had the opinion of the alternative health care that said get adjusted and your body would fix itself. That was true to a point but the fact was my body was so worn down for the infection I had that I wasn't healing. The other opinion I faced was that I should receive the healing that God wanted me to have. I felt guilty that I didn't receive God's healing because I thought my faith was so small and I thought I looked like a hypocrite. I had the surgery and it was the best decision for me. It was not because I didn't have faith to receive God's healing because I had the faith to receive healing many times. I did still get adjusted which allowed me to heal much quicker and for the first time in my life since I was a teenager I wasn't cramping all month long.

The best part is my best friend Barb stayed with me and helped me as I was recovering. She was such a blessing and a God send to me and she made the biggest sacrifice of all for me. Barb quit smoking while she was taking care of me. To me that was incredible because every time people would see Barb she would be drinking coffee and smoking cigarettes. That had to be the hardest thing for Barb to do but that is what makes Barb so special to me. Her heart is the biggest thing in her body and she would do anything in the world to help. Quitting cigarettes was really hard on Barb but she did it and I love her to this day and always will. Barb came through for me when I needed her most. I was healed and I could not have done it without her. When I was down about not being able to have kids she cheered me up and the fact that she put up with me while she was going through nicotine withdrawals really meant a lot to me.

Later on that year Jim and I got the shock of our lives. It was a hard year for everyone health wise. My dad had been in the hospital for his heart condition and had to have a valve replacement and bypass surgery. We were both scared that he wouldn't be able to make it. Jim's dad on the other hand was still the powerhouse of the family. He was very active in Rotary and had just been to Russia on Rotary and just returned in time to make a trip to Scotland after a brief intermission with his Granddaughter at Rockbridge. Nobody ever thought that one night a couple days after fathers day I would get a call from Jim's mom telling me that Jim's dad died in Scotland. He died of a fatal heart attack while attending a dinner in Rotary. He died in his boots just like he said he wanted to do. When Jim came home I was balling and he was balling and at first he was upset because he thought my dad died and then he was in shock when he realized it was his dad who died. It was the night before fathers day and I was doing a writing for fathers day and as I was sitting there I felt a cold wind in the room and I just barely caught a glimpse of a silhouette of what I think was his dad's spirit because the person I saw in the corner of my eye wore a hat that Jim's dad wore and a jacket he like to wear as well. A couple days after that Jim thought he saw his dad when he was talking to his boss and then he thought he saw him in the airport when he went to pick up his mom.

Jim and I both struggled with the aftermath and disbelief and shock of losing his dad. During that time we were blessed to have someone stay with us for a few months. God miraculously placed Jenny in our lives when we needed to grow the most. We had known Jenny since we started going to Life Christian Center and she began to stay with us during a difficult time in her life. Jenny was good for us because she taught us a lot about the bible, she was an inspiration to us because she was not afraid to witness to people. She was an encouragement because she loved the Lord and she loved studying the Word of God and she also helped us to see things that we needed to do in order to increase our faith.

After Jim's dad died I didn't know how to deal with the loss nor did I know how to deal with Jim appropriately when he needed me the most and I was desperate for answers. Jenny had told me about fasting and I had not fasted since High School but I knew more about fasting than I did when I was a teenager. I decided with the help of Jenny that I would fast until I got the understanding I needed to be a better wife and a better Christian. It worked in big ways I never would have expected. The results were "Most High Connections" our ministry that was inspired to be named after Jim's heavenly father who was in fact his living father. I also had visions during that time of Jesus feeding the 5000 and I was there watching him and at the end of the fast I had been inspired by the Lord to make a stew for the people at New Life Evangelistic Center which was a homeless shelter among other things to help the needy in St. Louis. I also gave them some bread. The meal fed everyone in the shelter that evening. After that we were blessed more than we had been in 10 years.

After Jim's dad died his mother decided to sell the apartment building and we needed to find another place to stay that would take dogs. Everyone agreed that we would be throwing money out the window so it was decided that we would own a home for the first time since we had been married. The financial blessing was unbelievable and we moved into our very first home November 1st, 1997.

In 1998 we faced our difficulties with victories and we overcame every difficult situation that came our way. The day after Resurrection Sunday Jim fell down the steps and fractured a bone in his foot that made him unable to work for three years. Fortunately at the time I was working regular so we were able to pay the bills. 1998 was also the year that the Lord instructed me to create my first book with all the writings I had ever done. In November 1998 we met Tim and Al (Morning Radio Talk Show Hosts at KJSL) for the first time who have played a major part in our spiritual growth. Since that time we have been introduced to some incredible ministries and found our passion to make this world a better place to live for all people.

In 1999 our spiritual muscles were stretched and our faith grew as we faced new challenges and overcame greater obstacles with blessings that could only come from God. We were doing better financially which was first of the much needed blessings that year which really helped when we faced the first test we faced that year. In may Jim's mom found out that she had lung cancer and she was having difficulty getting along by herself. For a long time we made regular visits to her house and did regular maintenance along with having family dinner's on Sundays which was as much of a help to us as it was to her. We ended up spending more and more time with her and helping her and in June we decided to move in with her because I was getting over extended as Jim's mom needed more help. That was one of most challenging times in our lives.

I am grateful for the opportunity to spend so much time with Jim's mom. Our relationship grew a lot in a few months. I grew to love her as much as I loved my mom. There were difficult times when we lived there as tempers flared and space was compromised with practically living out of boxes but we got through the hard times all the way to the end. It was during this trying time that God lit a fire in Jim's heart for what God called him to do. Jim has always had a passion to make this world a better place to live. He has seen the suffering and lack of caring and sharing and he wanted to be the answer. We did what we could over the years for different people who came our way but in October 1999 the Lord gave the answer to Jim's prayers. Jim had heard on the radio about a technology show that was being held that evening and Jim couldn't resist the opportunity to learn about new technology so we went to the show that literally changed our lives. Jim was on fire like I had never seen him before. He looked like he got struck with lightening. The next day he told his mom about what happened at the show and told her this is what God had called him to be a part of so she gave Jim the go ahead to take his stocks and invest the money in United Community Services of America. It hasn't been an easy road but the blessings have been incredible.

Jim's mom got her transfer papers to heaven on October 27 after three long months of Radiation therapy. Jim and I was faced with many conflicts as we could not move back into our home since the people that rented the house from us would not move out but at the same time we were being forced to move out of Jim's mom's house because we could not afford to live in that house or buy it. Family tempers had also flared constantly since the death of Jim's mom as well. We were accused of stealing jewelry that was given to me by Jim's mom while she was alive; that added to the aggravation when it was discovered that Jim's mom threw away some much treasured letters that her granddaughter sent them while she was a foreign exchange student in France. As traditional family relationships struggled our spiritual family relationships flourished and at the end of the year we were renewed physically and spiritually.

In the year 2000 we were blessed beyond the curse and the joy of the Lord gave us strength to move mountains. Our praises could be heard in everything we experienced. Every imaginable blessing happened to us in the year 2000. In January I was diagnosed with high blood pressure due to the stress I had been under with my job. We took a vacation to Florida in March and we had a good time and most of all I relaxed. A week after we got back from Florida I had another vision of the Lord. Jim and I woke up in a house of windows and we saw Jesus coming to the house and we opened the door to let him in and he said "It's a beautiful day to go fishing" so we walked to a nearby bridge and started fishing. Nobody caught anything for hours and it was getting late but just as we were ready to give up Jesus caught a huge fish and we wrapped it up and he said "Let's have food and fellowship together." We invited everyone with us and some strangers we ran into along the way. I had made some bread earlier and we were passing around jars of wine for everyone to drink and everyone was blessed and satisfied. Jesus then said "Let's go for a walk" so we walked with Jesus and saw some incredible beautiful scenery and I knew it was heaven because everything was perfect and we talked about things that were going on in our lives and how we didn't understand why we were suffering and he stopped and turned around and looked at me and he put my hand in his and he gave me five little stones and they were soft and shiny and they had pictures of heavens and stars and animals and he said "all this is yours as your inheritance and those things you are going through are only temporary light afflictions. Don't be troubled by what you don't understand and your joy will make things whole". When I woke up from the dream I was in a state of euphoria and I couldn't sit up and I smelled the most wonderful smell and I saw a cloud hanging over me.

    We had been spending a lot of time with our friend Tim during the year and growing in our spirit and our walk with the Lord and the Lord was really blessing us in many ways. One day as Jim was in the process of getting a new car and trading our minivan in since we had so many problems with it he was just getting ready to cross the street and he was just inches from getting hit by a car and something pushed him back. He didn't see anything or anyone that could have done that but he felt it. He did stub his toe and lost a toe nail from it but he walked away instead of hit by a car. Later that day he met Tim and I as we were going to a live radio remote together and we got to the Live remote just rejoicing that we were all alive and safe. They frequently gave away items at their live remotes and that day was my lucky day. They were giving away a basket of goodies including a coupon for a massage and 5 CD's and a bunch of books and two tickets to the "Women of Faith" Conference. I had been wanting to go for a couple of years and I never would have gone if I hadn't won the basket. We were showered with blessings.

    I went with Jim the first night of the Conference and then invited a dear friend Maria the next day. It was really a blessing for the both of us. Later on in the year I went to a C.L.A.S.S. Seminar which was like a writing workshop for people who wanted to make more of the creative abilities so I could figure out how to get my book published. I met with my Group Leader and she encouraged me about my writing and I left with some very helpful information. I realized I had a responsibility to share my writing talents and to pursue publishing my book.

    During the year we went to various churches with our friend and one church in particular that really moved us and made an impact in our lives. Spirit of Life Christian Worship Center was a little church with a big anointing. At first they didn't even have a church, they just met at a meeting room in a motel. It was so anointed that one day while we were worshipping Jim saw Jesus sitting right next to him and what moved him more was that Jesus told him not to worry because all would be well with him. Our lives have been dramatically blessed since that time and we are looking forward to whatever else God wants to do in our lives. There are more stories than what I have shared in this chapter but it is time to go treasure hunting again. It is my prayer that you will realize how God has worked in your life and how you can also be blessed with the treasures you find in the following pages. Enjoy!

TO RECEIVE FROM THE GREATEST GIVING GOD

To those who thirst and hunger for justice done.
In **Matthew 5:6** our God of justice is the only one.
From one who shows much giving of goodness.
The same is given in **Matthew 10:41** in likeness.
The greatest gift is the reward of giving one's love.
As we receive in **Matthew 19:17** the gift from above.
When we learn to give out of sacrifice for his sake.
Matthew 19:29 says a hundred fold is what we partake.
Faith adds a new dimension to the word receive.
For in **Matthew 21:22** you get what you believe.
That which you give in meeting other's needs.
Is that which in **Luke 6:36** is returned to you in deed.
Living your life to give of His Love is a blessing.
Luke 9 verse 5 is the way to keep it from passing.
Eternal life is the greatest reward to man is given.
To receive the gift in **Luke 10:25** the key is within.
All that we long to give Jesus for gifts such as this.
The will in **John 11:4** to give God glory is His wish.
The most permanent of gifts can not be taken
The gift of the Spirit in **John 14:17** is never shaken.
The treasure we seek can be blessed with joy.
When in **John 16:21** Jesus name is our given ploy.

For all that is received through the love of God.
Humbly should **Acts 2:38** be the path we trod.
When through our lives much gifts are received.
May we all find the key in **Acts 20:35** we believe.
Amen.

AN ODE TO BE SAVED

The Lord gave me a blessing today.
He opened by eyes and asked me to pray.
He wanted me to know that He is the way.
He told me I was weak but in Him I am strong.
No matter how hard I tried, I could not right my own wrong.
He showed me how I was bound by lies and sin.
But He is the Truth that sets us free from within.
He told me He loved me, that he died for you and me.
And that my sin was paid with His blood on Calvary.
His love gives us eternal life that we can enjoy abundantly.
He is there to take your strife and we can thank Him eternally.
He says he loves us, one and all.
Happy or sad, short or tall, with his love we can not fall.
When we open the door of our heart and let Him in.
He closes the door on our past sin.
He says to the poor in Him they are rich.
And He can feed the world with His loaves and fish.
To all who worship and tithe to the Lord.
He has proven true to return thirty, sixty and a hundred fold.
All we have to do is in Him believe.
And to love one another that we may receive.
Don't wait any longer to live without sin.
Open your heart and let Jesus come in.
If you have back slidden it's not too late.

You too will see God's heavenly gate.
He said He is faith and He will never leave.
Believe in Him and His grace you will receive.
Open your heart and just believe.
In God's Precious Holy Name I pray.
Amen.

VICTORY FOR YOUR SOUL

I have made a covenant to fill your soul so you can see.
There is no greater victory than found in **Isaiah 55:3**.
As the night brings darkness and the day brings light.
Matthew 6:22 shows the battle between sin and life.
In a world where life is an option and justice is a lie.
Let **Matthew 10:28** for your soul be your battle cry.
In a world where money rules and leaders are the foes.
In **Matthew 16:26** the greatest value is in our soul.
You can have the greatest gift that money cannot buy.
Matthew 22:37 is the price you pay for your new life.
Many tests and trials come as prayer gives way to pride.
Let **Mark 8:37** be your light that you never want to hide.
The battle for your soul is not fought with bomb or gun.
3rd John 1:2 is how the greatest victory is finally won.
This world seems very dark when life is full of sin.
Isaiah 30:18 shows us how to let the light of Glory shine.
The justice in this world may seem farther from the truth.
Let **Isaiah 61:8 &9** be the guide that leads our youth.
Life supplies more questions when we only seek the answers.
Isaiah 65:23 & 24 is the key for our lost sons and daughters.
We are given the option to live as such a gift has been given.
Matthew 25:34-40 is the example Jesus gives us to live in.
It is so important to remember that we are never in God alone.
For **Galatians 3:14** reveals the gift that makes us feel as one.

Love is not a mystery when found in it's sole creator.
Ephesians 1:3-8 is the formula that makes it last forever.
Trials and tribulations are seasons that soon shall pass.
Revelations 14:13 brings the peace that will last and last.
When it is said that good things come for those who only wait.
Revelation 20:6 is the exception when it comes to heavens gate.
If you learn one thing from this, I pray that it will be.
That it will cause a leap of faith so you will reign with me.
Come follow me the best is yet to be.
From your Heavenly father, Amen.

WELCOME THE HOLY SPIRIT INTO YOUR HEART TODAY

The Counselor of **John 16:7** which Jesus sent our way.
John 16:13 says let go of the cares of this world today.
As the special gift of the spirit can only show the way.
When the enemy comes against us and tries to cause dismay.
John 16:14 tells of the righteousness that joins us when we pray.
The gifts are not just given for the Holy Spirit alone.
1st Corinthians 12:7 shows we are joined together as one.
Not given in just one shape for size the Spirit comes to everyone.
As found in **1st Corinthians 12:8-10** it's a gift from the Holy one.
Find peace in knowing **verse 17** that whatever gift you have been given.
God have that gift with the Spirit to bless the Kingdom of Heaven.
How special we are to receive such a gift that brings pleasure to the Lord.
Even the least of these can be the greatest and by our Father adored.
So come one come all don't wait any longer.
The sooner the better will make us all stronger.
In the name of Jesus our Lord. Amen.

"Acts 2:32 This prophecy was speaking of Jesus, whom God raised from the dead, and we all are witnesses to this. 33 Now He sits on the throne of highest honor in heaven, at God's right hand.

And the Father, as He promised, gave him the Holy Spirit to pour out upon us, just as you see and hear today."

THE GIFT OF GRACE

Only a gift so precious and perfect can be given by God.
like in **Psalm 84:11** where obedience for His Glory trod.
What beauty surrounds the light of such a gift as this.
As shared in **Joel 2:23** where His rainbows of love assist.
Yet the gift far greater than gold or pearls of the sea.
When **Acts 6:8** show the blessings that you receive.
Great is the gift that He saves for even the least.
And for all in **Acts 20:32** He provides even a feast.
The benefits are quick but the joy lasts and lasts.
For in **Romans 6:14** our past stays in the past.
It is an awesome gift just for what you believe.
As in **1st Corinthians 15:10** your strength is retrieved.
Goodness and Peace will nourish our troubled lives.
As **2nd Corinthians 1:12** replaces the trials of our minds.
As we grow to receive His Gift more and more.
2nd Corinthians 4:15 is what our Savior longs for.
We can all be a part of God's Masterful Plan.
In **2nd Corinthians 9:14** He can use a mere man.
So when we receive such a gift we feel not worthy of.
We can live like **Galatians 2:21** in the spirit of love.
The ways of the law will not see you through.
Let **Galatians 5:4** be the lighthouse for you.
So what treasures are found from God's Might Heart.
Titus 2:11 is a great place for eternity to start.

The price is far greater than the wealth of the world.
Hebrews 2:9 delivers through love greater than words..
Don't wait any longer for this time shall pass.
And in **Hebrews 4:16** our benefits will surpass.
The payoff is great and it's a dream come true.
2nd John 1:3 is that He wants to see happen for you.
Let the precious gift of God's Grace bless you today.
In Jesus Name we sincerely pray. Amen.

CHAPTER 3

IT'S ALL ABOUT HIM

It is my desire to give glory and honor to God the Father, Jesus the Son and the Holy Spirit. Without God who gave me life through my mom you would not be finding Hidden Treasures. Without Jesus there would be no inspiration to write about the glorious salvation that bring me such joy and peace. Without the Holy Spirit I would not even be here today because He kept me from following my own will for my life and keeps me grounded on the will of God. This book would not even be worth reading if it did not give you an awe of God and what He has done and what He can do not only for me but for everyone who is not afraid to open the treasure chest of blessings God has intended for them.

One of my favorite sayings is "you only get out of something what you put into it". Our relationship with God is no different. I have seen people who lead good lives and not even have a relationship with God and they won't even get to live in eternity because they think they are good enough. They will not get anything but eternal death. I have seen people who go to church on Sunday and sing songs and listen to a sermon and go home and put their bible on the table and go on the rest of the week in their other life without God. Those people also lead good lives and live happy and they even enjoy the message of love God has for them but that is all they will get. I have seen people who love God and read His Word everyday and pray and give thanks and praise to the Lord and tithe and they are blessed. Everyone at church knows they are a Christian but they don't shine so others can see God working in their lives. Then I have seen the people who are sold out for God and they live their lives as the light of the world to shine for all to see. Those people believe in healing for their bodies and receive it. They believe in financial blessing and get it. They have strong marriages and happy families and good jobs because they not only know the hidden treasures but they live them out in their daily lives.

Jim and I have gone from glory to glory through the years. We have grown from the 2 hour Sunday People to the tithing and reading the word of God. Now we are the sold out for God people who are receiving the fullness of God's blessings in our lives. We have always been blessed even when we just went to Church on Sunday or watched the Hour of Power and became Eagle Club members. God never holds back his blessings because of how we live our lives since it is not by works that any man should boast but because of His Grace. It is not what we do that causes God to bless us but it is God's love. We just discovered the secret that when we please God with our faith it pleases God to give us everything. There are times when his grace has been sufficient and we thank him for that because if we only praised God for what He has given us we would never be happy enough. We would not be happy with one house and one car and one TV but we would have to two houses and a butler and a maid and a million dollars so we wouldn't have to work. We are truly rich and we don't have a whole lot of money and we have one car and we both work but we live to show the riches we have in Christ. That is the real treasure and our real reward. If you take away God from our lives we are an empty shell. It is my wish that you will want the treasures in life that God gives so you will feel as blessed as we have. The following is a Collection of Love Letters of God. Enjoy. Just remember wherever you are in your relationship with the Lord there is no condemnation in Christ Jesus.

THE NAME YOU CAN TRUST

When troubles look big and the future looks dim.
Genesis 1:1 and **Psalm 19:1** will lead you to *Elohim.*
The same God of power and might is the *God* who is supreme and true.
When we seek the words of **Numbers 23:19** He is eager to see us through.
Exodus 6:2 and 3 shout the glory of God's precious name divine.
Just a breath of *Yahweh* brings a sweet spirit and peace of mind.
Nothing more sacred could we ponder than the name of *El Elyon*.
What better way to celebrate than with **Psalm 7:17** in a song.
Oh how blessed shall our lives be as in **Genesis 16:8** *El Roi* is deemed.
When you feel hope is lost your suffering too has been seen.
Psalm 91:1 is the place not found in likeness of a shelter or nest.
Fir it is in the name of *El Shaddai* where shadow gives you rest.
Fear not for needs you see not met in this troubled hour.
Just hold fast to **Genesis 22:13** for *Yahweh Yireh* is your tower.
When the end seems fast approaching and precious time seems lost.
Resound the name *Yahweh Nissi* as **Exodus 17:15** is betrothed.
When the world seems filled with wonders and jewels that catch your eye.
Hold fast to Deuteronomy 6:4 which reveals the awesome *Adonai.*

When world events begin to take it's toll remember them all in prayer.
Remember **Psalm 59:5** and know that *Yahweh Elohe* Yisrael is there.
When the threat of murder and violence begin to attack your faith.
Yahweh Shalom in **Judges 6:22** is the light that will guide your way.
When you see the war in other nations and all seems lost of respect.
Keep in mind that in **Isaiah 1:4** *Qedosh Yisrael* alone is perfect.
As the battle goes on with evil principalities and powers yet undone.
Let us sing harmonious to *Yahweh Sabaoth* of **Isaiah 6:1**.
In times when all seems so uncertain as even good things fall away.
When we look to **Isaiah 40:28** we can know *El Olam* is here to stay.
Surely as our imperfections fail us and sin eats away at our soul.
Rest in *Yahweh Tsidkenu* of **Jeremiah 33:16** for he is righteous alone.
Not one thought lost, no need unheard, or good deed will go unnoticed.
For *Yaweh Shamma* of **Ezekiel 48:35** is always here among us.
As it was in the beginning and so shall it always be given.
Highest Praises to *Attiq Yomin* for whom **Daniel 7:13** was written.
May the highest honor and praise be given to the one for whom this is written.

CHARACTERISTICS OF FAVOR WITH GOD

Noah had favor before Jesus came.
A man of righteousness and had no blame.
Hard to achieve but he kept his obedient heart.
Walking with the Lord, God have him an ark.
(Genesis 6:8)

Joseph could have lived without understanding.
Sticking through the tough times, God have him better landing.
(Genesis 40:14)

Favor with God meant much more to Moses than life of mere existence.
When God showed him more than mercy, kindness, and goodness.
(Exodus 19 and 20)

Nehemiah was one who saw and sought the favor of God.
For Nehemiah longed to walk the paths in those the Lord would trod.
(Nehemiah 1:11, 13:31)

Job's understanding of favor with God was gained with fear and respect.

Hidden Treasures

God liked what he saw in Job's heart and gave more than Job would expect. (**Job**)

Psalms was the book of much favor and lack thereof.
From pleading hearts of God's kindness to a mere glimpse from above. (**Psalm**)

Proverbs listed the expectations to receive the precious gift desired.
From loyalty and kindness to humble honest goodness transpired.
(**Proverbs 3:34, 11:27, 16:15, 18:22**)

After all has been said to earn such a blessing.
It took God's love to show what was missing. (**Isaiah 61**)

The Lord gives favor with whomever pleases him.
But he rejects the offerings of those who appease him.
(**Malachi 1:9**)

When it seemed all was lost and his favor was gone.
It was found in a child, his one and only son.
(**Luke 4:19**)

His favor is greater than that of the past and lasts into the future.
With greater gifts that silver and gold, he is our kinsman redeemer.
(**Acts 15:11**)

This new favor we have sets captives free and cause the blind to see.
Not given by works of goodness but through Jesus we only receive.
(**Acts 4**)

Greater things have been offered to have just a hint of this blessings.
But only those who stay true in the world will experience the joy within.
(**Acts 11:22**)

No other gift can keep on giving as the one we most often seek.
But it's what we do with what we are given that makes the blessings peak.
(1 Corinthians 3:10, 15:10)

To harness the power in such a gift would be a greater sin.
For the gift has greater power when we let the spirit in.
(2 Corinthians 12:9)

CAN YOU HEAR ME?

I know it isn't easy in a world of war and chatter.
But there is one still small voice who's impact is much greater
    (**Deuteronomy 18:15**)

The people in the time of Moses had this problem too.
But I still dealt with them no less as I will do with you.
(**Exodus 6-16**)

Although at times I have shown my wrath on those who turn
    against me.
I am only fair and just and proven generous with my love and
    mercy. (**Numbers 12**)

Surely you listen to people who can lie in times of adversity.
But how much harder is to listen to one who is true throughout
    eternity. (**Numbers 23:19**)

Everything that is heard from me is meant for you to trust.
I have never made a covenant without leaving something to entrust.
    (**Genesis 9:11**)
(**Deuteronomy 5**)(**Hebrews 12:14-15**)

Even though you listen it is in your heart to know I am true.
If you trust and obey when you hear my voice, my goodness will
>   dwell in you. **(Deut 6:3, 7:12)**
A curse can turn into a blessing in just a moment of time.
A decision is the link between fear of death and peace divine.
>   **(Deuteronomy 30:15-20)**

I listen for your voice and also hear your request.
So find peace when fear abounds and know I offer rest.
(2 Chronicles 7:10)

There is restoration and victory when you listen to what I say.
And know that I am with you as wickedness and evil come your
>   way. **(Job 22:22, Psalms 5:2,3)**

Offerings from your heart with praises and joyful song.
Will bring me much more pleasure than a gift from doing wrong.
>   **(Psalm 40:6, 58:2-4)**

Wisdom doesn't come from watching others fall.
It comes from hearing the God who knows us all. **(Proverbs)**

Not one word that I have spoken has failed to come to pass.
As you listen to my words, know as my covenant my words will
>   last **(Isaiah 7:14-16)**

For all who are willing to listen I will make their understanding
>   clear.
If you get your wisdom for hearing my voice you will have no
>   reason to fear. **(Acts 38-41)**

And so it is written from Genesis to Revelation.
All who are willing to hear should listen to what the spirit has to
>   say **(Revelation 2:29)**

Let me close by saying this...
Psalm 46:10, 11 "Be silent, and know that I am God.

I will be honored by every nation.
I will be honored throughout the world"
The Lord almighty is hear amongst us, The God of Israel is our fortress. Amen.

IN JESUS NAME

When hope seems lost in the sea of humanity.
Stand firm in the redeemer of **1st Peter 1:3**.
When fear overtakes you with war in your midst.
Come to the prince of Peace of **Isaiah 9:6**.
While travel seems difficult and the way seems amiss.
Let your eyes find your guide in **John 14:6**.
As all other treasures in life fail the test of time.
You can know eternal love found in **Romans 8:39**.
When you ears long to hear the sweetest chime.
May your heart know the voice of **John 5:25**.
In times of humble weakness as troubles seem too great..
May you find the greater strength in **Hebrews 7:28**.
For times of struggle where sin and sorrow abide.
Rejoice in the Spirit of **1st Corinthians 15:45**.
When the bread of the world leaves you hungry and dry.
Fill your life with the sweetness of **John 6:35**.
As you fail to see the pleasure of fame and wealth.
Let your heart find its way to **John 8:12**.
While the world eats away at your self esteem.
Be sure in the promise of **Revelation 22:13**.
It is my greatest hope when all is said and done.
That you will have the life of **Revelation 15:1**.
Amen.

A FOREVER FATHER

Dear Father God.
    As you know Fathers day is coming soon and just so you won't feel forgotten I wanted to share a gift from my heart that was made out of my love for you.

Matthew 5:10-12 reminds us we're here for a reason.
And You are there to help us through every time and season.
Mark 14:36 must have been hard as your son suffered distress.
But only you could make that call to save a people like us.
What joy you must have felt when in **John 15:9** your son shared
    your love.
If only we can honor that love with our praises raised to heaven
    above.
Our lives are so lost with out your wisdom which is what your
    word is for.
Only good can come out of a marriage when we turn to **Matthew
19:4**.
Thank you for teaching us how blessings come as we respect your
    holy request.
As we learn to honor our parents which **Ephesians 6:1** reflects.
The greatest gift that could ever be given was given by you by your
    mercy.
Let us never forget the pricelessness of your love in **1 Peter 1:3**.

Let us all humble ourselves by the example you gave through **John chapter 1**.
So that every day will be celebrated Fathers Day as we are joined in your son.

P.S. If there is anyone who does not know you as father and hears this gift, let them receive you right where they are so they can be blessed with your eternal gift. Amen.

THE LIVING REDEEMER

Oh Blessed Redeemer greater than all.
You give your life to cushion our fall.
Bring us back to the heaven in deed.
Our kinsmen redeemer for all who believe.
(Leviticus 25:25)

In days of Ruth you gave blessing to faithfulness.
After a time of great trial you gave her soul rest.
(Ruth 3:9,10) (Ruth 4:14)

Let your hearts ring out with the spirit of Job.
As we remember the stand You took on our your oath.
(Job 19:25)

Harness our words and humble our hearts.
As we stand on the rock that sets us apart.
(Psalm 19:14, 78:35)

May we always remember your heart so true.
so unworthy we are to be thought of by you.
(Isaiah 41:14)

For not only redeeming us from what we have done wrong.
You redeem us from the wrong of others till we sing your victory
    song.
(Isaiah 43:14)

Knowing our blindness to the light that you give.
You guide us along when it's for you that we live.
(Isaiah 48:17)

We stand in awe of the price that was paid.
To be chosen to live so that we might gain.
(Isaiah 49:7)

With your anger you could have killed us all.
But thanks to your love, we can answer your call.
(Isaiah 54:5-8)

Thank You doesn't seem quite enough to repay.
For redeeming us, loving us and giving us each day.
(Isaiah 60:16..)

O blessed Kinsmen Redeemer and Most Holy Lord.
All glory, honor, and praises be raised to You in one Accord.

A SACRIFICE

Let us offer **Psalm 27:6** as a gift for your might Protection.
As we humbly share Psalm 40 verse 8 in complete submission.
Let Zion be filled with your beauty from **Psalm 50 verse 5**.
As the praises of your people are sent to you Mist High.
Let our broken and contrite hearts be made right today.
As **Psalm 51:17** is made true in our lives when we pray.
May our songs and prayers of Thanksgiving be heard.
As the sacrifices of **Psalm 107:22** is joyously offered.
Let the world be our witness as we declare your matchless glory.
While **Psalm 116:18** is reflected in telling your story.
Make our heartfelt prayers be made as those in **Psalm 141 verse 2**.
As your joy can be felt with praises we offer humbly to you.
We welcome the wisdom of **Proverbs 21:3** in our eyes.
So better will our praises be in the offering of our lives.
Open the eyes of our heart to seek your will in **Matthew 9:13**.
so we can openly share your Mercy to those who have not seen.
Lord, let our sacrifices be received as graciously as the one you made.
As we remember **Hebrews 9:26** and worship you for the price you paid.
Since once for all our debt you erased and we stand before you free.
Hear the words of **Hebrews 10:12** as we now humbly decree.
May the Glory of your name and your presence rise among us.

And let your truth of **Hebrews 10:14** be heard by all those around us.

Let us now sacrifice our highest praises for the one most worthy of our praise.

And may our prayers of Thanksgiving and worship for **1st John 2:2** be raised.

Amen.

GOD BE WITH YOU

Through many times you have to me with loving heart and bended knee.
Find comfort in **Deuteronomy 31:8** my saints and know your prayers touch me.
As troubles and trials have come against you and you bellowed out my name.
Isaiah 43:2 and 3 are just for you to show your cries to me are not made in vain.
When your life seems void of meaning and your future causes you to fear.
It is in the midst of your uncertainty that **Philippians 4:9** will make thing clear.
Those times when you felt weary from doing the best that you could do in life.
1st Chronicles 22:11 is the thought for the day that will give power against all strife.
In every time you come to me and wonder if I will come through for you.
It is my wish that in **Genesis 28:15** you will know that every word I promise is true.

CHAPTER 4

BLESSINGS FOR ALL PEOPLE

Out of all the times that Jim and I have been blessed in our marriage most of the time the blessings came just in time to get us out of a mess or kept from getting hurt or healing when we were sick or meeting people who really blessed us. Sometimes blessings would come in spurts and for long periods of time His grace was sufficient when we thought we could have been blessed more but one time in particular that stands out among the rest in that we got an overflow of blessing in the midst of what most people would consider a tragedy. This oddly enough occurred while we were on a long overdue vacation that we didn't get in August of 2001. God turned a vacation from hell into a vacation of supernatural blessing.

The trouble started early in the morning when we were leaving from St. Louis. We were all packed and thought we had everything we needed and we got to the airport and we were waiting in line like everyone else. We waited and waited and found that we were in the wrong line and that we should have been on the inside because we were going to be vacationing outside of the United States. We got inside the terminal and it was about 20 minutes before our flight was scheduled to leave and they told us just to take our bags and go through the terminal and check the luggage in when we got to the departure gate. We got to the gate about 3 minutes before the plane was scheduled to leave and they checked us in and told us our luggage would make it on the plane and just to get on the plane.

That was the first miracle that happened considering we could have been sitting in line for another half hour and would have missed the flight altogether. We were on the plane and on our way to Florida where we would catch another flight to the Bahamas.

We arrived in Florida and got off the plane and we had no clue where to go or what we were supposed to do as far as getting to our next destination. It was a good thing that we had an hour and a half layover. Jim decided he could not go any further till he had something to eat and I was getting nervous because no matter where we looked or who we asked nobody could tell us where we need to be and the people at the check in desk never told us we needed to pick up our luggage. We had the understanding that our luggage would be enroute to our next departure gate. We finally found somebody who knew where we needed to go but it was at the far end of the terminal and we were 15 minutes away from our next plane was taking off. We made it to where we need to be and we got on a bus with our carry on luggage that we had lugged from one end of the airport to the other and we made it to customs where they checked our documents showing citizenship and then they called us to stand outside and get ready to board the plane. It was blazing hot and we stood outside for a half hour and people were getting upset because they were getting sick so they let everyone come back in and sit down while they figured out what the problem was and found out that the pilots didn't realize they were scheduled to fly out. They finally figured everything out and they started getting the luggage on the plane and told us we had to put our carry on luggage in the baggage department and we didn't think to check our other luggage we thought it was already on board because we were told our luggage would be there. We got on the small plane and it was much louder than the first and it vibrated more so I was a little more nervous on that plane but we landed safely in Grand Bahamas Island.

We got off the plane and grabbed our carry on luggage and we made it customs where we were asked to fill out some paperwork and we didn't have a pen and they wouldn't give us one so we looked around till everyone was almost gone and somebody let us use their pen and we finally got the paper work done and they checked our documents and then they let us go to the baggage claim area to pick up our luggage. We waited and waited and we never saw our luggage. Another couple also had a problem with their luggage and we made a report of it and the people in the baggage claim area said they would track it down and they would send it to us when it got to the Island but they gave us a number to call in case we didn't get it by that evening. We flagged down a taxi and told them where we were going and we were on our way to the motel. We were a little concerned about the luggage but we were not going to let it ruin our day we were just looking forward to enjoying our vacation in the Bahamas. We got the key to the room and we went up to our room and took showers since we had been hot from waiting outside for the plane and we took a brief nap and Jim was up and about looking for necessities like places to eat and a bank and a grocery store so we could buy food.

When Jim got back I was ready to go and we went down to the lobby where we met Mama Rose. She was the first of many wonderful people we got to know personally from the Bahamas. We first wanted to find out where a church was because we wanted to go to church while we were there. Mama Rose asked us what kind of denomination we were and we told here we were Non Denominational and we were hoping to find an anointed church that preached the word and believed in the Holy Spirit. She recommended her son in law's church. She told us she wouldn't be able to go because she had to work the next day but she would make arrangements for us to get a ride to the church the next morning. Then we asked her where we would find a store so we could get some groceries and she said there was one not too far away and she offered to take us there if we could wait about an hour for her to get off and she offered to show us around a little but while she dropped off her friend at home. We spent most of the time just having a real nice conversation with Mama Rose until she got some customers and we walked around a little bit looking for a place to eat. We were starting to relax and when we got back to the motel Mama Rose was just about ready for us and we left. She drove by the store and showed us where it was and she said she just needed to drop off her friend first and she was going to go home where her son could take the car and give us a ride to the store.

Mama Rose showed us the different churches and buildings and she told us some interesting things about the Bahamas. She talked about their government and how getting a loan was so expensive their that a lot of the houses we saw were partially built because people would add on and continue building when they got the money to do so instead of getting a loan to fix it up. She also said that 95 percent of the people were Christians and that is why there were so many churches. I think we drove by 33 churches on the way to her friends house. After she dropped off her friend we went to her house and she showed us around and showed us her garden in her back yard and I was surprised at how much such you could grow on an island but everything was doing very well. She gave us some sugar apple which we never had before and it was different but it was good and she gave us some lemonade while we waited for her son to get ready. After her son got ready she told us to enjoy ourselves at church and she would see us Monday. Her son gave us a ride to the store and we were getting ready to pay with our travelers checks and found that Jim didn't give me the travelers checks but the receipts for them so we could not use them and they didn't take debit cards so we had a little bit of cash and we just bought some rice milk and raisins and a small box of cereal and we got dropped off at the motel. We put the food in a cooler and went down stairs and we were told our luggage still didn't make it and it was getting late so we proceeded find a place to eat since it was getting late and Jim had to eat. We found a restaurant and everything was crowded and we finally got to eat at about 10:30 then we walked back to the motel. They accepted credit cards so we were in luck there. We got back to the motel and still no luggage by 11:30 so we went to bed and hoped we would get it the next day.

    The next day we got up and we had about an hour before we were going to get picked up to go to church and Jim went looking for a place that had some clothes we could wear to church since our clothes were beginning to smell in the mean time I was on the phone with the airlines trying to figure out what was going on with our luggage. Jim came back and told me to put on something he picked out for me and he liked it and he got himself a shirt and we waited in the lobby for the ride to church. Mama Rose's daughter picked us up and we found out that her husband was the pastor of the church. We really enjoyed the service. It was a small church that reminded us of Spirit of Life Christian Worship Center in St. Louis. They had testimony and scriptures and praise and worship and then the sermon. We introduced ourselves to the congregation and asked for prayer because the airlines had lost our luggage. Everyone was so nice to us and I think we talked with everyone for at least another hour after the service before we got a ride back to the motel. The pastor gave us a ride and we talked about our ministry and Pastor Bernard was very nice to us and we asked about other services and told him we would like to attend his Wednesday Night Bible Study and we said a prayer together and we looked around for a place to have lunch because it was about 2:30 when we got back.

    I got back on the phone with the airlines and they told me they could not find the luggage and I started to panic. We needed our clothes and asked them what we were supposed to do and she said they would issue us a voucher for $150.00 for clothes if we kept the receipts. Now we were having to pay for all our food and buy clothes but at least we had a certain amount of money in our checking account but we would not have money to buy anything extra. I went up stairs to take a nap in the room after the crisis on the phone with the airlines. and Jim went looking around for some things to do on the island. Jim did find a pair of swimming trunks so we did a little swimming while I was resting. When he got back we went looking around for some more clothes and tried to find a swimming suit for me but with no luck and it was getting time for dinner so we found a less expensive and quieter place to eat. On our way to the restaurant there was a choir singing in a performing area of some sort and they were getting everyone all happy and dancing around and it was a blast to be a part of it. We took a lot of pictures with our camcorder which we had a lot of fun doing. After dinner we spent a long time walking around and we found a beach near by so we walked along the beach after dark and we went back to the room.

    Monday we woke up and had breakfast and talked to Mama Rose and told her about how our luggage was now lost and we just blessed her because we told her we would not let it ruin our vacation. We had made reservations for a tour that day and just as were

Hidden Treasures

getting ready to go Jim realized that we didn't have the ticket we needed to get on tour but Mama Rose talked to the tour guide and got it worked out and we were on our way to get a tour of the Island. We first stopped at a historic botanical garden that had animals and a neat tabernacle church and we took a lot of videos of fish and waterfalls and beautiful birds. Then we drove through millionaire row where all the well to do people lived and then we stopped at liquor store for some rum sampling and then we went to the market place where there were a lot of shops. We finally found a swimsuit I could wear and we found an ATM so we got some cash so we wouldn't have to keep using our card and we wanted to go to the store to get some more stuff for breakfast. We were at the place where were told to meet the bus driver and it started raining so we were heading for cover and we ran into a building where there was a timeshare and we started talking to them and we told them we already had a timeshare we didn't like and we were trying to get rid of it. They gave us their number in case we changed our minds and they offered us a free lunch if we came to a demonstration. The rain stopped and got on the bus and got back to the motel. I got into my swim suit and we went down to the pool and we went swimming for a while and Jim thought we could just get some hamburgers but they were too expensive so we found another place for lunch and I got my peas and rice and Jim had to try the conch salad since he had heard so much about the natural Viagra. After lunch we went to the beach and basted their for a while then we went back to the motel to make reservations for dinner since we got a coupon for a free glass of wine and a free dinner including transportation to and from the restaurant. We didn't get picked up till about 9:00 and then they had to pick up a couple other people and God had his hand in our lives again. We found out the one young couple just got married and they were spending their honeymoon in Bahamas and were talking about our 14 years of happy marriage and the other couple got picked up was just getting married the next day. They were a little older and it was their second time around but we were witnessing and blessing everyone. We got to the restaurant and we ordered. Jim got his first taste of grouper and he really liked it. There was a lot of time to wait for dinner so everyone sat outside and we gave them so gospel tracts and everyone was enjoying themselves and we got back to the motel about 12:30 and we were to tired to go for a walk after dinner so we just went to bed.

Tuesday was really a relaxing day, we stopped by and talked to Mama Rose and Sister Brenda and asked where we might be able to find a bank to replace the travelers checks and we found out there was only one bank at the other end of the island and they would be closed by the time we got their and they couldn't even guarantee they could do it so we gave up on that idea. It would cost us more money to take a taxi there and back and wouldn't save any money at all so we just decided to take it easy that day and just go swimming and stuff. Before we left, sister Brenda asked me to reach out my hand and she gave me some money for us to have lunch with. I humbly accepted and thanked her sincerely and she had to help some other people so we left and we were rejoicing and thanking God for his goodness. I got another beach type dress and Jim got some more shirts and we went swimming in the ocean and I got burned so we had to go to the drug store and found some aloe and I went back to the room and rested till dinner time and we at dinner at a Greek restaurant. We went back to the room after dinner and the power went out and it started raining so we just took it easy the rest of the evening.

Wednesday came and did a little swimming but I didn't do a whole lot because I was still hurting from the sunburn. We talked with Mama Rose and Sister Brenda and Mama Rose talked to one of her friends that worked at a timeshare place that gave free T-shirts and free lunch so we took her up on it since we didn't have anything better to do. It seemed like no matter what we did or where we went were given the opportunity to bless people. Our representative who showed us around was a real sweet lady who was taking care of her grandmother and she was really blessed as we talked with her. She just never saw such a wonderful couple that was so kind and encouraging and she was glowing the whole time she was with us and we kept telling her that we could not afford to get another timeshare even if they sold our timeshare and by the end of 4 hours they finally decided they couldn't help us and told us a shuttle bus would pick us up in about an hour. They dropped off our free T-shirts later after we got back to our motel since that is what they offered us from the beginning. We got back to the motel and Mama Rose had already gone home but she left a message that she would meet us later at the prayer meeting and that they would pick us up around 7:00. We went to eat and got back to the motel about 6:30 and Pastor Bernard picked us up and gave us a ride to the music minister's house for the prayer meeting. That was the most awesome meeting we had ever been to. The Holy Spirit was all over the place. Everyone was praying and rejoicing and I was just on fire with the Holy Spirit and they put a fan right in front of me and gave me juice because they were worried I was getting too hot. Pastor Bernard gave a real good message and after that we sat around talking and I couldn't help but notice a beautiful picture and I commented on it and found out that the music minister's son did the painting and I talked with him and encouraged him and told him to keep his dream about attending Oral Robert's University as he wanted to be a minister. Then before we were getting ready to leave The music minister's wife asked me if she could see my purse and she put 30 dollars in it and I thanked her graciously for it. After Pastor Bernard dropped off Sister Brenda he dropped us off at the motel and he was asking about our luggage and we told him they lost our luggage and he said he would stop by the next day and get us a few things that we could wear till we got back to the states. He would not take no for an answer so we agreed to meet him the next day at 10:30. He took us to a couple of places and I got a shirt and pair of shorts and underwear and a nice dress. Jim got some nice Bermuda shorts and a nice shirt and they went to another store to pick up socks and underwear. Then Pastor Bernard dropped us off at a beach while he did some work at a construction sight. We really had a good time taking videos of the kids and the sea gulls and then Pastor Bernard picked us up and we were going to pick up Mama Rose at the Medical Center where she was getting some tests but she wasn't even done yet so Pastor Bernard just dropped us off at the motel and we were hungry so went to dinner and we walked around and we were just in awe of all the incredible things God had done for us on this trip that the devil meant to use for harm. We were more blessed than I think we would have been if we hadn't lost our luggage. We were more grateful for the fact that we could still stand and praise God and thank him for everything even in the midst of chaos.

We didn't get to see Mama Rose until Friday which was the last day we had to spend in the Bahamas. We told her how concerned we were but we were glad she was there and that she was doing okay. Mama Rose was not done with us yet, she had looked around for something to do for us since we didn't get to spend any money on souvenirs or anything so she arranged for a complementary trip on a glass bottom boat so we could go out in the ocean and see the coral reefs and stuff. That was really neat and we had a great time. I even saw a shark that was finishing off a fish. That was so nice of her to do that. When we got back we thanked her again for everything before she had to leave and we said our final good-byes because we wouldn't get to see her the next day. After we said our good-byes we went upstairs to our room to start getting ready to go the next day and we went out walking on the beach and we signed up to go snorkeling in the coral reef. Jim thoroughly enjoyed it and we saw a huge queen angel fish. We ended up being the last ones out of the water. After snorkeling we got in our clothes and went to our favorite Greek restaurant where we said our final good-byes there to the restaurant owner and their waitress who was going back to college the following week. We got a picture with them and then we spent the remainder of the evening. Taking in the sights and sounds as they were celebrating a surfing competition the next day. That night when we got back to the room I could hardly sleep, my sunburn was hurting and I was so pumped by the awesome time we had in the Bahamas and the Lord gave me a writing at 2:30 in the morning.

The next day brought yet more challenges that we were not expecting. We went to the check out desk at the motel and we started checking out. We found out that we had to call for a taxi to get us to the airport and we also had to pay 12 dollars for a phone call we made from the room and we had 36 dollars but that was it so we didn't have the US currency we need to leave the Bahamas. Jim went to every ATM he could find and none of them were working and nobody had US currency. Then Jim remembered that we were supposed to get a voucher at the airport for the clothes we had to buy and we found out that they wouldn't be there for a couple of hours so now our plane was going to be leaving soon and there was no way for us to get cash to leave the country and I started to panic. Then the gentleman at the check in desk at the airport said he would pay the money for us to leave the country and he said it wasn't necessary but if we wanted to pay him back he gave us his address. I was shocked. The devil's final attempt to ruin us failed and we shouted victory yet again. We returned to the United States and we were out of money and Jim went looking around for the place to get the voucher we were supposed to get for the clothes and they only gave him $36.00 because most of the receipts were hand written by straw markets which is where we got most of our clothes and they wouldn't accept them. The whole time we were there was spent running around from one place to another then we couldn't get the check cashed then it was time to get on the plane back to St. Louis. We did get to eat on the plane which made Jim feel a little better but naturally our nerves were seared by the time we got to St. Louis but we made it and I found the guy who was supposed to pick us up and we finally found Jim at the baggage claim area and we went home.

When we got home we found the place a mess and the guy who stayed at our house to watch the dogs messed up a pan and warped the counter top and killed our sea star but he left before Jim could confront him about it. In a way we were not surprised to be confronted again with the devil's attempt to break us but over all that happened we still look back on that vacation and we still rejoice and thank God for making it the best vacation we ever had next to our Bermuda Vacation. We did get our luggage back about a week later. Somehow it ended up in Houston Texas. We have never been on a plane since that time and if we ever do we are taking our carry on luggage only and we will never leave without our bible and our faithful love for God because God is the god of all of our life and when God is with us nothing can stand against us. If there is anything I want you to get from this testimony it is that every tragedy or crisis you face in life is not the time to blame God for not being there or for letting something bad happen but it is an opportunity to thank God for the blessing and victory that is going to come out of your faith that will grow in times of struggle.

DEAR LORD
(PRAYER FOR THE UNBORN)

Dear Lord,
I thank you for the precious child that you have created out of your love.
I thank you for loving this child and for creating it's existence from heaven above.
I thank you for giving this child a chance to live a life you mean to be.
I thank you that you wanted them to be part of your family tree.
I thank you that you gave your child a mother who can love them the same.
I thank you that you will love this child no matter what sin is to blame.
I have a wish for this mother who may or may not know you.
That you have placed this child in her because your love is true.
Let her know it wasn't a mistake and that you knew what you were doing.
You loved this child and made it for her before she knew it was living.
Show her that no matter the sin that made this life come to pass.
You want this child to have a chance and it doesn't reflect the past.
For in you who created all things have created this child as well.

And let this mother know in her heart that you don't make things
from hell.
(Leviticus 18:21)

Let her know that this living child inside her womb is capable of
loving too.
Because this child was created for bringing peace and giving
praises to you.
Let her know the promise you made that they have the right to
inherit.
That you offered them this world so they could be a blessing in it.
(Psalm 25:12, 13)

Please don't let this mother rob your blessed child from life in
glory.
so this child can share the blessings of a wonderful living story.
But if this mother is cold in her heart and robs you of this life.
Please love this child on her behalf till we join them has heavens
wife.
And please teach this woman the forgiveness you have so she can
have eternal life.
Amen.

HEAR THE PRAYERS

I heard a prayer for you today.
That you would choose to go my way.
I created that child you hold inside.
And I chose you to mother with pride.
I didn't make this child as a punishment to you.
But that he or she could have a chance to bless you.
I heart a prayer for a woman today.
Only she decided to go the wrong way.
Her baby didn't have a chance.
To play, to laugh, to pray, to dance.
The angels cried for innocent blood that was shed.
But I still love and forgive that mother instead.
She could have been a nurse who cared for others.
He could have been a minister to care for single mothers.
Will you find it in your heart to heed to one who prays.
So my child living in you will bless you in many ways.
There is no reason to be ashamed of what the Lord has done.
Just rejoice in me each day for the life of your little one.
Love Your Heavenly Father.

DEAR MOTHER OF THIS CHILD TO BE

Will you hear these words from me.
This child you carry is not a mistake.
I created this child for my hearts sake.
This child is a blessing believe it or not.
I never made a child I didn't want.
I didn't make this child to die so soon.
I just saw a glimmer of hope in you.
This little life is a source of great joy.
Giving back much more love than any toy.
A girl or a boy whatever the color.
Deserves a chance to be loved by a mother.
No one ever said it would be an easy road.
Bit if you turn to me I will help carry the load.
Before you make a tragic choice today.
Just remember that answers come when you pray.
As for this child whom you cannot hear.
Just think of the love that I hold so dear.
You have many people who are praying for you.
In hopes to make your child's dreams come true.
No matter the problem there is still another way.
And you can be a hero to this little child today.

Dear precious little child within.
I hope I gave given you a chance to win.
If I fall short of this goal today.
Remember I love you every step of the way.
There are many who are praying for your life.
But whatever happen I will give you eternal life.

Love Eternally, Your Forever Father

P.S. People are waiting and hoping this true message of God will encourage you to choose life for your unborn child. They are willing to do anything to give your child a chance for life. Let them give you and your unborn child a chance today.

John 16:21 and 22 When her child is born her anguish give place to joy because she has a brought a new person into the world. You have sorrow now, but I will see you gain, then you will rejoice and no one can rob you of that joy....

DEAR LORD
(A PRAYER FOR HURTING PEOPLE)

As this is the day we set aside to life you up and exalt you.
Let our lives be touched forever and our hearts for you be true.
As we sing praises and thanksgiving to your holy name.
Let every day we live our lives testify to the same.
As we pray for those who are in need.
Let their soil be ready to receive your seed.
As our hearts go out to those in the street.
When they see our face let it be yours they meet.
As we find those who are hurting from wounds so deep.
Let us given them a healing that their hearts can keep.
When we come across those who only know sorrow inside.
Let us show them the joy that in knowing you cannot hide.
As you anoint us to build up your heavenly kingdom.
We ask that you bless us with your eternal wisdom.
We thank you for the spirit you so graciously gave.
Let us use that gift so that more can be saved.
As this day goes by and evening comes upon us.
May the blessings of your glory forever shine within us.
Until that day when we see you face to face.
And we can forever praise you for your glory and grace. Amen.

DEAR LORD
(A PRAYER OF RESTORATION
FOR ALL PEOPLE)

We humbly come to you with our hearts which once rebelled against your truth.
(Hebrews 3:15)

And ask that you turn our rebellion against the sins that once separated us from you.
(1 Peter 4:1)

We gratefully thank you for your act of reconciliation that we no longer bare our sin.
(Romans 5:1,2)

Teach us to be your ambassadors, that those around us may also be reconciled within.
(2nd Corinthians 5:20)

Let us forever remember your love and mercy that makes us better in our regrets.
(2nd Corinthians 7:10, 11)

Replace the remorse in our hearts till our spirit of faith, hope, and love are set.
(Psalm 51)

Thank you that the world rejects us for all we do but you still stand by our side.
(Romans 8:28, 38)

Please give us a bold faith to stand in sinful rejection with your love we cannot hide.
(Hebrews 13:5, 6)

Thank you Lord for our repentance that even cause angels to celebrate.
(Luke 15:10)

Lord teach us to take our repentant heart and make this world a better place.
(Luke 19:8, 9)

Thank you for giving us everything for only in you we can see such glory.
(Revelation 4:11)

Let us take heart in respect of others so they can rejoice in your story.
(Romans 12:10)

We sincerely accept the responsibility of love for all in light of your holy request.
(Mark 12:29-31)

Teach us to be grateful for your gifts for us that all will see and be blessed.
(Romans 12:6-11)

Thank you that when we come to your place of rest, our spirits learn to fly.
(Isaiah 40:29-31)

Open our hearts to release to you all that burdens us, for in our faith you abide.
(Matthew 11:28)

Amen.

A PRAYER OF BLESSING FOR ALL

This is a prayer of blessing for all to know and hear.
To give you grace in your passing and a badge of courage in time of fear.
I pray for peace to give you rest.
I pray for strength to face each test.
I ask for provision in your time of need.
I ask for favor with all you meet.
A hedge of protection when enemies come.
A spirit of light when darkness comes.
A glimmer of hope when all seems lost.
A fountain of joy in time of loss.
I pray **Psalm 23** in time of uncertainty.
For **John 3:16** to set you free.
For **Philippians 4:13** to do his will.
For the Lords Prayer that you know still.
For **Philippians 1:21** when evil comes.
And that you pray in faith that God's will, not yours be done.
In Jesus Name, Amen.

CHAPTER 5

BLESSINGS OF OUR KING

It doesn't take a lot of faith to believe in miracles but without faith you cannot receive them. Jim and I have accumulated more than a mustard seed of faith and we attract miracles in our lives. Miracles are blessings that God enjoys giving when He sees his people grow in faith. God is a loving father who loves to give good things to his children. Faith is a no brainer for us because we have seen what faith does. The next testimony is a true example of what faith will do when that is all you have.

In the end of the year 2000 we had faced some incredible difficulties. I had lost a good job with insurance benefits and I was back working for temporary services. At the time we had a timeshare and we were scheduled to go to Arizona in November. We got every worked out and found a baby-sitter for the dogs and Chad and the fish. We were in the middle of our vacation and we had to return early because our zoo keeper couldn't stay the whole week which turned out to be a good thing we did. When we got back I did not get any temporary jobs so I went about two weeks without getting any income. It got to the point where we didn't have any money in the bank and I wasn't getting any checks from anybody. We were to the point that all we had was faith that God never let us go without food or shelter or anything we needed and we believed he would deliver us out of this situation as well. Our diligent faith paid off in a way we had never seen before.

Hidden Treasures

We had been regularly attending Spirit of Life Christian Worship Center that met at Howard Johnson Motel every Sunday morning. We were not going there to ask them for help because we just didn't do that especially since they had such a small congregation and they couldn't even pay for a church. We just went to feed our faith. We still had food in the cupboards but we needed food for our souls. We went to church that morning and God was waiting for us and ready to reward us for our faith. The praise and worship was especially anointed that morning. The most loving spirit was on everyone in the service. The message was flawless and we were blessed and thanking God for his wonderful and powerful word. After the message they took the offering and all we had since we didn't have any money in the bank and we couldn't write out a check was $1.67 in change. I remembered about the widows mite and gave all we had.

Then the pastor was asking for prayer requests and normally I don't raise my hand or ask people to pray for me because I am humble and never ask anybody for anything but this time I raised my hand and out of obedience to God I explained our situation out of desperation for an answer to prayer and knowing how when two or more are gathered Jesus is right there in the midst. That morning the church was rejoicing over the fact that they found another building so they could be able to accommodate more of a congregation. We were just rejoicing along with everyone and they had made an announcement that they were inviting everyone to lunch and to see the new building and they dismissed the service. Everyone just continued to stand around and had fellowship and we were not expecting what happened next.

One lady that was sitting in front of us in the service asked me if she could see my bible. I thought that was an unusual request but I gave her my bible. Then the music minister came up to me and asked me for my phone number because the thought there was a possibility that he would be able to find me a job where he worked. He then asked me if I was going to have breakfast with them and I told them we just gave all we had in the offering he offered to pay for our lunch and we accepted the invitation. Then one of the people in the congregation came up to me and he held out his hand as if to shake my hand and when I reached out my hand to shake his he put $46.00 in my hand and I could not believe it. Nobody ever did that before. The real shocker was next when we left to go to the lunch with everyone I got into the car and looked in my bible and the lady that took my bible put in $100.00 in it. We could not stop rejoicing and praising the Lord and thanking God for putting us in such a wonderful church family. We had lunch and saw the building and we mentioned that we were believing for God's anointing over the church since it was at one time a place of prostitution and drug dealing a long time ago. They all agreed to pray as well. When we got home that night we got a phone call from the music minister and he asked me if I would be able to go to work the next day. I told him I definitely could and he gave me the directions of where to go and he told me to be there at 7:30 in the morning and to ask for a supervisor and told me I could start working that day. It was not a temporary job it was a permanent job and never thought I could be more blessed than I was that day. Then about a week later we got a check for $1000.00.

Since then God has turned $25.00 tithes into $5000.00. I am looking forward to see what he will do with a monthly $58.00 a month tithe. I am believing we will be completely debt free before the end of 2005 and enjoy God's overflow. It is not easy to have the faith that the old widow in the bible had or the lady and her son who made bread for Elijah when they were thinking it was going to be there last meal before they died but that faith has some real blessings attached to it. Just as God has done for us with that faith so he will do it for you. God is such a loving father and He is just waiting for you to ask so he can bless you. In times where the blessing is just grace it can be more than sufficient for you when you know where you could be without his grace. For me there is no other option. I hold fast to my faith and embrace every opportunity to use it because I know what faith does and I love it. I hope you never run into the situation we had when we had no money in the bank but if you do I pray that you will give all you have in faith and watch you miracle grow.

A RIVER OF PRAISE

As the people of Christ are made one.
Let **Romans 15:5** for God's glory be done.
When the walls of difference fall.
Let **Romans 15:7-9** be scriptures for all.
As we humble our stand with one another.
Let **1st Corinthians 3:9-16** join our spirits together.
Let us find the link to each brother and sister.
As **1st Corinthians 12:24-27** bring us closer.
Let us know the value of Jesus in our lives.
As **Ephesians 2:20-22** come first in our minds.
Let our hearts remain strong with open spirits.
As **Ephesians 4:3** quenches us as we receive it.
What blessing and glory we will see.
When **Philippians 2:2** is the gift we believe.
Awesome is the power of His precious love.
When **Colossians 3:14** covers us from above.
Let our hands be raised and our voices sing praise.
As in **Psalm 47** releases our spirit of faith.
Let our words fill the air with great joy.
For **Psalm 85** in our hearts employ.
Let God be pleased with our offering gift.
As He receives the fruit of **Psalm 133:1-2** from us.
May the blessing of our faith be remembered.
As the bonds of **Matthew 18:19** can't be severed.

As we rejoin together in the highest heavens.
Let us look on these times **Matthew 24:31** rescinds.
When all is said and done in front of God we stand.
Let joys of **Luke 15:6** be sung throughout the land.
Let these last days be filled with gratitude.
As **Acts 10:9 and 10** form our final attitude.
Until the day when to Jesus we say.
Thank you for blessing us all the way. Amen.

THE FINAL REVIVAL

The cries for revival have long since been seen and heard.
In **Psalm 119:25** it comes through knowing the Holy Word.
Fear and discouragement flee from the Protector we heed.
2nd Chronicles 20 shows reform that calls God to answer the need.
As sin corrupts and we are blinded to seek God's Holiness.
Numbers 6 gives the key in rededication to purify our unruliness.
When all the lands have heard The Word and the works of good are downcast.
Find comfort in **Ezekiel 29:21** when the word revival will forever last.
At times when emotional strength is lost and you thirst for the quenching flow.
Refreshment is found in **Proverbs 11:25** when you share that others may know.
As we prepare for the feast to come let our hearts be made humble and new.
For hearts that are resembled in **Isaiah 57:15** are made fresh as morning dew.
In process of making our hearts ready for God's glory to shine on our days.
Hebrews 9:26 calls us to remember His Son who shows us His Holy Ways.
   Where is hope for the weary in these days of senseless war.

Acts 15:16 shows the rebuilder of souls is never very far.
In a day where compromise is an excuse to live in a sinful peace.
Let **1st Corinthians 5** be the sword that slays the evil beast.
When our hearts are cleaned and God's love is clearly seen.
Psalm 51:10 will cause revival and make room for His Glory within.
When the days of revival have come and gone and the clouds have disappeared.
Psalm 126 is the hidden oasis that remains for those who hear.
In search of a lasting revival to answer the prayers of the saints.
By the words of **Luke 24:47** let our voices be heard in cadence.
Let these glorious days of Holy Revival rain heavily on us all.
And let the words of **Isaiah 40:29-31** keep us standing tall.

In the presence of His Spirit for such a time as this.

WHAT A BLESSING IT IS

For God is the giver from which all blessings come.
Like the blood that He gave from His Precious Son.
His love and grace are worth far greater than gold.
With **John 3:16** salvation reveals many blessings untold.
When curses seem to be the norm and relief seems far away.
Matthew 5 is a looking glass for the blessings you see today.
In **verse 1** God gives us the key to what blessings means when he taught on the mountain side.
Just when you feel your hope is lost, He shows how your gifts will not be denied.
In **verse 3** when we see our weakness and in need of a helping hand.
He gives us the kingdom of heaven as our promised land.
In **verse 4** as we come to an hour of grief and despair.
He seeks to relieve us as he offers comfort there.
In **verse 5** As we face times when we feel helpless and weak.
He Promises blessings from valleys to peaks.
In **verse 6** as we start to have doubt in the ways of the world.
He gives complete justice for all who have heard.
In **verse 7** when we learn from the Lord in what we should do.
Our mercy is blessed for His Mercy is forever true.
In **verse 8** Through years gone by and wisdom is learned.
God blesses our seeking with His presence we yearn.
In **verse 9** in times of war when all you long for is peace.

God adopts you with blessings that will never cease.
In **verse 10** the evil we face in the times our faith stands.
Will all pass away but blessings will stand in His Holy Land.
In **verses 11 and 12** from those way back and to those who will follow still.
Blessings are promised where faith abounds God will never fail.
God has blessings for us that we can never conceive.
It hardly seems faith that we first just believed.
How do we bless a God so wonderful and worthy of praise.
We can begin with **Psalm 103:1 and 2** in all of our days.
Blessings are meant to be shared when passed on to each of us.
Isaiah 65:16 shows the rewards when we speak in whom we trust.
There was a beginning but there is no end to the blessing God gives each day.
In **Hebrews 13:21** with His glory and grace let us share with others along the way.

In grateful dedication and devotion to our wonderful source of blessing.

FORGIVENESS

My heart was grieved with an enemy.
As unforgiveness kept me from Calvary.
As the blood of Jesus cried out "Forgive".
It was shed for our sins so we can freely live.
God makes it clear that it's not without price.
Matthew 6:14 and 15 gives fool proof advice.
When **Luke 17:3 and 4** are performed in us.
Only then can we say In God We Trust.
If we follow the wisdom of **Matthew 18:22**.
Then our savior can say our forgiveness is true.
When **Ephesians 4:32** is the theme of our nation.
What will our enemies think of our salvation?
When people are hurting and cursed with disease.
Will **Mark 2:9** be the cure that sets them free?
How much longer will our children's hearts grow?
If **Romans 12:17 to 19** is the foundation they know.
What would our war torn foes of hate have to say?
If we manifested **Ephesians 4:2 and 3** as we pray.
As we are encouraged to live a peace filled life.
Let **Luke 6:37** be our tool against war and strife.
What an awesome responsibility we are given.
When **John 20:23** speaks of those not forgiven.
As we submit our hearts to the Lord in prayer.
May the fruition of **Colossians 3:12 to 14** be there.

We give our prayers with **Mark 11:25** believed.
So we can share with others the blessings received.
As we come to you with humbled hearts today.
Let **Hebrews 12:14 and 15** be heard when we pray.
Thank You Lord for your forgiveness every day. Amen.

THE HONOR TO LIVE ON

Let us give honor to whom it was received from.
For to be like the Father we must live like the Son.
May the honor be learned with the purest of heart.
With our faithfulness in prayer our spirits will never part.
Teach us Oh Lord to be true to **Romans 12:20**.
So that not only our eyes but others see Your Glory.
As we learn from the words of **1st Corinthians 12:23**.
Fill our spirits with the Joy of **verse 26** that it brings.
Lord know our hearts to right in all we pray.
So that **2nd Corinthians 8:21** will be done in what we say.
In as such that is told in **Philippians 4: 8 and 9.**
Let us know the peace and grace of your glory divine.
What more can we say to give honor and praise.
Than that **1st Peter 2:12** is the life that we humbly raise.
To You, Oh God and to Your Son and Spirit be the greatest glory forever more. Amen.

AN OFFERING IN STONE

Lord I come as a living rock of faith to you I humbly raise.
Let me stand strong and firm with words of Highest praise.
I lift up to you a sacrifice of everything I have, or say, or do.
Just let me be a blessing as my spirit come wholly to you.
You live in me and shine through me and your live in me abounds.
Let all the words and songs of my mouth come out like holy sounds.
Let my witness be greater than the seed that withers away.
Let my rock be used as your fortress where faith can firmly stay.
Thank You for planting the seed in my life in which I now stand tall.
Let me be an example to others that by your mercy will never fall.
Thank you for **1st Peter 2** in which these blessings were written.
Let all who receive and hear these words know from whom it is given.
I give you all glory and honor for all you have given and will give through word gave to me.
                            Amen.

CHAPTER 6

GOD IN ALL THINGS

One thing I have learned over the years is that God is ever present in every season of our lives. Good and bad times alike are times when God is patiently waiting for us to notice the blessings He gives each day. It is easy to see God's presence in good times because we are blessed with sunshine, beautiful flowers, caring friends, and wonderful parents. Even when it is not easy to see God's presence like times of war, murder, abortion, crime, unemployment, debt, divorce and terrorism, God is still here. One instance stands out in my mind more than any other time when 9/11/01 changed countless lives for better and worse but God was a major influence in the lives of many people during and since that time. In reading this chapter I hope you will see and Thank God as well for what He has done in all our days.

At 8:11 am on 9/11/01 I was on my way to work and listening to the radio and then I heard the devestating news. Flip Benham, who was being interviewed by our friends Tim and Al was watching it on TV and he said he could not believe what he just saw. The first plane hit tower number 1 then the saw plane number hit tower number 2. I suddenly felt trapped and helpless in my car and wanted to get out and stop everything because something more important was going on. I kept my composure but still shaken and wanting to ball my eyes out. I needed answers and my first cry was out to God and asking him in desperation what was going on. I kept on looking up in the sky thinking it must be the time when Jesus is taking us away from this sin cursed world. That time never came. I made it to work and I called Jim. Jim was still sleeping and he didn't even hear what was going on. I told him to turn on the news and that the World Trade Center Towers had been hit and then I heard about the towers collapsing. My supervisor came in with his radio and turned it on and it seemed like the whole world stopped what they were doing as their eyes were fixed on the events in New York.

Minute by minute the gory details were coming in about the terrorists plot and the attacks in Washington D.C. and the other plane where they didn't make their intended destination but wondering what was next. The world seemed like the last place I wanted to be and I cried out to God "let this be the time to take us home". Obviously it wasn't our time but it was time for those in the towers and on the planes and the building in Washington D.C.. It was also the time for many people to stop what they were doing and consider where they stood and what they would do in this time of disaster. As the hours went by there was no light in the world. There was no goodness, just despair and hopelessness. I could hardly wait to see Jim at lunch time. He got to my work and I nearly leaped into his arms. We found a more secluded place and we parked and we started to pray. I was sobbing and Jim had the news on the radio and I just turned it off because I couldn't listen to any more. We both just sat there silent and I was crying out to God and telling him I needed answers. I needed to know why this was happening and what I was supposed to do now in this time of crisis. I asked the Lord for his peace and in an instant he gave me an instruction I had never thought I would hear but in obedience I counted all the chapters from Genesis 1 till the 911th chapter of the bible and it came to Malachi chapter 4 which is the last chapter of the old testament and the chapter before Jesus comes in the new testament and I read it and I found answers.

My fear stopped and I found direction and a focus to end the chaos of the moment and to restore the sense of brotherhood. It seemed that during that time many other people were finding their way to restore brotherhood in the world as well. I started hearing about people who where running to try and help someone else.

There were special Church services on the TV and radio and offers of people to gather together and to pray for our nation. All of the sudden the focus was not on the wickedness but on how to find light in the dark world and the nation was turning to God and His direction for such a time as this.

We went to church that night. We couldn't think of being anywhere else. It was during that time the Lord was starting to give me the words of my writing "Why United We Stand". It was an awkward time for the church but we unanimously called out to God for President Bush, and other leaders in authority. We started praying for the families of those who were lost in the towers. We were praying for people every where in the United States who were lost that they would come to the lord. The next day when we listened to the news were heard of people surviving the disasters but also many who died. We watched in awe of the destruction and the fire and the clouds of smoke and piles of rubble and people lined up one behind another desperately hoping to hear a cry. We saw firemen tirelessly working and picking up peace by peace of rubble looking for signs of life. We saw many people with food, water, supplies, face masks, chairs and cots for firemen to rest periodically. We saw brotherly love and support for those who serve to protect us. We saw love for others and saw others seeking love. We saw people turning to God for their hope and understanding in the situation. Not just people in New York but all over the world. People remembering how people in the United States always reached out a helping hand and now the world was coming together to reach out to us. There was a spirit of sadness but also a spirit of thanksgiving and love. 9/11/01 was not a good time but good things came out of it. Many people sought to renew a relationship with God. Many people reached out in love to others. Brotherly love was a responsibility and not just a saying anymore.

Along with the brotherly love and goodness of men there has been more attacks on human life than there ever was. As much goodness abound so does the wickedness of the world. Like 911 days later when trains were demolished and terrorism stuck out it's ugly head to remind us that wickedness was not going to go away just because we proved to fight against hate with love. Even though a lot of the evil still exists that was there before 9/11/01 but the people are different. Even though the brotherly love is not as evident as it was in the months following 9/11/01 it still exists and as long as there is breath still left in this soul I will yet praise my God and thank Him for teaching a big lesson about our relationship with Him. Even though evil and hatred is still present, peace and love still abounds. I still to this day love others, pray for others and seek ways to help others when I can. And I thank God that He is there every day, hearing my prayers and loving the unlovable and still shining a light in this dark world.

WHY UNITED WE STAND

I have heard the cries of people all across the land.
Deuteronomy 7:23 and 24 are your cue to take a stand.
I have heard the questions why, and how and what do we do.
Exodus 14:13 and 14 hold the answers to what I will do for you.
When things begin to scare you and peace gives way to fear.
Remember **2nd Chronicles 20:9** and know that I am here.
When you start to feel alone and want to run and hide.
2nd Chronicles 20:17 will be the truth to keep you brave inside.
When enemies come in battle, don't lose sight of faith.
Ephesians 6:13-18 will give you strength to run this race.
Look not on what seems to be great loss in hatred and strife.
While **Galatians 5:1** reminds you of the gift we have in life.
Be encouraged in your faith not wavering in troubles that come.
As **2nd Samuel 22:33-37** affirms the victory when we stand as one.
Forget not what has brought you this far as a great and godly nation.
As **Matthew 12:25** shows you the consequences of separation.
Look on ahead now to the future that is promised in my word.
Revealing the truth of **Isaiah 48:10-13** to those who have not heard.
Stand confident in your salvation and proud in what you believe.
While **1st Corinthians 15:58** bestows the blessing you will receive.

Lift yourselves up with the promise in the hope that you possess.
Finding comfort in **Isaiah 14:24 and 25** to give you peace and rest.
As you come to me in prayer this day humbled on bended knee.
Let the truth of **Isaiah 7:9** be the weapon your enemies see.
To God the be Glory the inspiration of His Word. Amen.

PEACE FOR FREEDOM

I have watched you on the news for hours at a time.
Wishing I could tell you that everything will be fine.
I don't know you personally but I love you just the same.
Man or woman, white or colored, a hero without a name.
Even though you fight for freedom half a world away.
The love we hold in our hearts for you will never stray.
As you catch a glimpse of the country you proudly serve.
Let not your heart be troubled by hatred you have heard.
I say a lot of prayers for the peace you vow to defend.
And struggle for peace when it brings lives to an end.
I only know a peace that I am longing for you to have.
Found in **Colossians 1:20** with the blood of just one man.
When darkness fills the sky and you long to see a friend.
Let **Luke 1:76 to 79** be the light that guides to till the end.
As people may not see the cause for which you strive.
May your heart find strength with **Micah 5 verses 4 and 5**.
You may not see the purpose of battles you may face.
I hope **Romans 5:1 and 2** will give you hope to run the race.
While the spirit of war may seem like it's tearing you apart.
Find **Ephesians 2:13 and 14** and bring healing to your heart.
Before you embark on the journey you've been asked to trod.
Let **1st Timothy 1:1 and 2** keep us linked together with God.
I may never see you in person to give you a great big hug.
But I hope you keep in your heart the peace of God's love.

Sincerely proud of you (our troops) and proud to be an American.

9/11 VICTORY PRAYER

Let us pray with the armor of love that victory may be our song.
Praying with the Angels and Saints in unison to defeat all evil's wrong.
Let us pray with confidence as we stand in strength and courage.
While others who are suffering will see our light and be encouraged.
Let your kingdom be filled with our righteousness and be declared glorious.
As we pray with your belt of truth to continually guide and inspire us.
Let the beauty of your love fill our lives as we are renewed and blessed.
As we pray hope for the lost and dying with your armor of righteousness.
Let us stand firm with shoes of peace that can only be found in your word.
So when we pray for others the message of your Good News is heard.
Let our hearts not waver behind the shield of faith which we stand.
As we pray in power and night for the healing all across the land.
Let the lost be found and their hope be seen as they seek your holy face.
When we crown ourselves with the helmet, the gift of your saving grace.

May all our words be spoken with mighty power and authority.
As we pray the gifts of the Holy Spirit to give honor to your majesty.
Lord hear our humble prayers what we pray with our hearts today.
While we bear witness to your Holy Light that guides us along the way.
We thank you for blessing each one of us with your precious love divine.
And for letting us be a part of the abundance in your harvest time.

May all Honor and Glory be given to your awesome, mighty, wonderful, precious, holy name we pray. Amen.

Inspired from **Ephesians 6:10-18**

THE BELIEVERS VICTORY SONG

As His kingdom we are the saints to serve God for His Glory Forever.
Let **Revelation 1:6** be the command of our hearts as we stand together.
As heirs of Gods glory and honor called to win the lost He also loves.
Let **1 Peter 5:2** be the catalyst to serve joyfully for our Kingdom above.
Thank God as He fills our lives with faith and love as He gave us the gift to share.
While **1st Timothy 1:12** brings us the humble reminder of why we care.
Let us remember the power of Gods grace and mercy as the blind begin to see.
Proclaiming **1st Thessalonians 1:5-10** that brings healing to those who believe.
Let us stand confident for what we stand and believe as we walk in the armor God.
With **Ephesians 6:5-12** to strengthen and protect us where the evil trod.
Let us not lose sight of the truth that gives us freedom to choose God in whom we serve.
Being reminded by **Galatians 5:13-14** of the law that all nations observe.

Let our gift of righteousness be the power that gives victory over the death of sin.

Living by **2nd Corinthians 6:6** as we show others the peace that comes from within.

Let us be encouraged to win the race set before us as we become heroes of the faith.

Encouraged by **1st Corinthians 16:13-16** to endure the greatest tests we face.

Let our joy be complete when we serve the Lord united in love for each other.

Declaring **Romans 14:17-19** as battle cry that keeps us standing together.

As the things of this earth grow dim in the light of Gods glory and grace.

Let our Victory Cheer be the sound that brings the lost to seek His face.

CHAPTER 7

A GOD FOR ALL SEASONS

It is my hope and intention that you have been blessed in what you have read. My love is genuine for all people. It is an honor to share the gift of writing the Lord has given to me and I believe He gave it to me just for you as I mentioned in chapter one. This book is for you whether you love poetry or hate poetry. Whether you are a Jew, or Christian, or Catholic, or a nonbeliever this book is for you. This is not something I have always dreamed of doing so I could become famous but to give Glory to the Lord and to bless everyone so they can give Glory to the Lord. This book is all about Him. My life is all about serving Him. Without Him there would be no book. If there is one thing you get of out of this book I hope you find a new joy, peace, and love for God and His Word (The Bible). I hope that you will take your time and meditate over the scriptures that you find in my writings and you will enjoy the treasures revealed in this God inspired book. If you have been blessed or if you have questions about what you have read. If you would like me to speak with your congregation or group. If you want to find out how to become a part of Most High Connections I want to give you the opportunity to contact me. This book is just an abbreviation of what God has done for me and what he wants to do for you. The best is yet to be.

You can email me at:
jchmhc2you@sbcglobal.net
You can call me at:
(314)428-8386

WELCOME TO A PLACE CALLED HEAVEN

Just open your heart and your spirit will see.
The place in **Isaiah 57:15** in store for you and me.
This place is not made for the unclean heart.
But if you follow **James 4:10** you will leave the dark.
The message is clear of the blessings of heaven.
As **Matthew 5:3** shares the heirs to whom it is given.
If greatness is the treasure your heart longs for today.
Matthew 11:11 will guide your narrow way.
For those who are wandering and choose not to hear.
Revelation 22:15 is the message that is painfully clear.
But God is a merciful and wonderful got you see.
You will find in **James 2:5** He longs to bless you and me.
Beyond the highest mountains far greater than the sea.
Find **Matthew 13:41** and see no death or sin's slavery.
The work is not finished but the final days are soon.
As **Matthew 13:33** calls us to shine brighter than the moon.
It is not by what we do that will decide our eternal fate.
But by the attitude of **Matthew 18:4** that makes you truly great.
The kingdom is now and it's king will reign forever.
If you live your life by **Matthew 16:19** your blessings are never severed.
Such a precious experience not one to be taken lightly.

For only those who know Jesus in their heart will be honored to see His Glory.

A MESSAGE OF HOPE AND UNDERSTANDING

Thank you Lord for seeing us as your created us and not for our understanding.
We also thank you for teaching us the key to your understanding.
May you be honored by our desire to do your will in loving one another.
Let your blessings fill our hearts as we desire to comfort our brothers.
Let us treasure the gift of your faithfulness in times of weakness and sorrow.
As you put a nugget of faith in our hearts to give hope in all our tomorrow's.
We thank you that your precious gift is far greater than gold and silver.
Your light shines so bright to guide us and the fruits of your love will never wither.
So in all these things in faith we know this sorrow too shall pass.
And that we may grow in understanding as we look forward from our past

Inspired by **2nd Timothy 2:11 - 13**.

THE GIFT OF TIME

As time doesn't seem to be such a gift any more.
I hope this gives understanding to God's gift forever more.
Whenever you hear **Ecclesiastes three**.
It is my wish that you find it's truth that sets you free.
You were born to bless the world with your presence.
As there is time for dying to leave the world your essence.
Planting times and nurturing soil bring forth natures beauty.
While uprooting timely weeds that rob your life of plenty.
Killing thoughts that harbor strife, resentment and pain.
Healing your spirit restoring contentment and gain.
Tearing down strongholds that leave you weary and dry.
Building up streams of joy and hope that eternally satisfy.
Weep as willows in passing of those who brought you joy.
Laugh at past adversity while in victory you now employ.
Mourn for a while as tears cleanse the soul.
Dancing for joy in the refreshing eternal flow.
Scatter stones in times of transition.
Gathering stones during times of submission.
Embrace the gifts enjoyed with goodness of friends.
Refraining from conflicts of foes and passing trends.
Search your heart for your destiny to impart.
Giving it to Jesus when it bears heavy on your heart.
Keeping memories that remind you of your success.
Throw away the bad times that bring hurt and distress.

Tear down the walls that leave you in bondage.
Mending fences that grow weary with homage.
Be silent when chaos abounds and know His Voice.
Speak boldly when you know the other choice.
Love life with all your heart and soul and might.
Hate that which robs other the freedom of sight.
For wars and rumors of wars will come in time.
But only peace will come in The Glory Divine.
From the giver of the gift. Amen.

YEAR OF DEDICATION AND DECLARATION

I light my life as a candle to you this year.
As **Matthew 5:15** will in my spirit adhere.
I proclaim your victory with love and power.
As I know in **2nd Timothy 1:7** can not cower.
I dedicate my life to letting others see You in me.
For what I read in **Luke 11:36** is what I want to be.
I want to live the example of **1st John 1 verse 7**.
So I can encourage others in looking towards heaven.
Let my life please you as I have learned in **Isaiah 58:6**.
So I can be seen in your eyes as a good witness.
Let my heart resemble **James 1:12** each day.
As a path of light for others who may come my way.
I want to live my life as seen in **Matthew 4:16**.
So other hearts will see the day of **Matthew 5:16**.
Let my life be tried and tested in **Isaiah 8:20**.
So other souls will not be lost by what they see in me.
Of all the things I most desire of all your words I read.
I hope to someday hear the words of **Luke 19:17**.

LET GLORY REIGN ON THE YEAR OF YOUR HOLY ONE.

As we reflect on the blessings of God's Holy Son.
Let us remember the love that made us all one.
As we look on the gifts of **Ephesians 6:23**.
Let us bless the Lord with our will for peace.
As we rejoice in the promises of **Hebrews 8:6**.
May we shine His light that the lost won't miss.
As our eyes are opened to the truth of **Ephesians 1:13**.
Let us give the praise called by God for these things.
As we are faced with days that don't seem to go our way.
Let **Matthew 6:33** be our peace and comfort each day.
As we talk our talk about the riches waiting in heaven divine.
Let us remember to keep our strength as mentioned in **Galatians 6:9**.
As we celebrate the blessings with dancing until dawn.
Let **Deuteronomy 2:7** be the theme of our victory songs.
As we strive to live our very best to make things right this year.
Let the words of **Psalm 37:5** be encouraged in our shouts of cheer.
As we approach the anniversaries with joys of years gone by.
Let **Ecclesiastes 9:9** be the reminder that true love will never deny.
As we look to find the perfect way to make the year complete.
    If we live our lives as in **1st Corinthians 1:4** we can never claim defeat.

Psalm 84:11 says it best when we face the coming year. When we live each day with God leading the way we never need to fear.

THE YEAR OF SPIRITUAL EYES TO SEE

As we come together in prayer for rulers and kings and those in authority.
Never in history has there been such a time to reveal **1st Timothy 3:16**.
Being called to stand as one for the cause and freedom of truth.
Our hearts should be ever so wary of the words in **Ecclesiastes 7:2**.
As the world brings to mind the uncertainty of things which are to come.
May wisdom and comfort be manifest where **Isaiah 63:11-14** is made known.
When fiery trials of life surround us and the world leaves us empty and dry.
Let **Romans 8:18-21** be the quenching flow that leaves our hearts satisfied.
As each day we live brings us more chances to share our eternal light.
Remember **1st Corinthians 2:7-10** which gives us reason to shine so bright.
Taking each step in faith on the narrow road we have chosen in life.
Counting it all joy as **Philippians 3:18-21** carries us past the valley of strife.

As we plan for time well spent with family and friends by our side.
Let the words of **Ephesians 1:11-14** be the treasures we abide.
Wake up each day with joy and singing joined with thanksgiving and praise.
Being encouraged by **Romans 8:29 and 30** to keep us strong in all our days.
As we start this year with expectation of a fresh new lease on life.
Let our hearts be etched with **1st John 3:2 and 3** as we seek our paradise.
The greatest gift we can receive is the hope given in the words we believe.
With the eyes of our heart fixed on the greatest of these let us find **Psalm 73:17**.

THE PERFECT GIFT FOR CHRISTMAS

In a time when many gifts are exchanged.
Will you thing of the kinds where lives are changed? (**Acts 3:5**)
As we search with our hearts for people to share.
Will our recipients know it's because we care? (**Romans 4:4**)
As we walk the streets that glitter and shine.
Will you remember the one who gives you peace of mind? (**John 14:27**)
As you ponder the gifts in which you will receive.
Will you remember the giver that made you believe? (**Ephesians 2:8**)
Are your finances low and your list seems high?
Did you know there's a gift that will never die? (**John 4:10**)
When you are making your list of guests to invite.
Will you thing of the children who need a home tonight? (**1st Chronicles 16:3**)
It doesn't take much to give gifts from your heart.
And the blessings from God will never depart. (**Matthew 6:2**)
The gifts that only money can buy will surely pass away.
But the gifts you give with joy in your heart will bless them every day. (**Romans 12:7 and 8**)
There are forgotten people begging for a piece of bread.

Will you give them living water so their souls will be fed.? (**1st Peter 4:10**)
There are people in need of a blanket and cheer to keep them warm this year.
Would you share contentment and love that will last throughout the year? (**Ephesians 5:16**)
There's a place in the world where broken hearts go.
Will you lead them to the place where healing waters flow? (**Proverbs 25:14**)
There is a country in need where war is fought.
Standing for freedom will you give them a thought? (**Leviticus 7:29**)
When the season starts to take it's toll.
Remember the gifts that renew your soul. (**Matthew 23:19-22**)
There are gifts you can give that will be worth while.
You can bring hope for the lost and bless a child. (**Luke 6:38, Psalm 127:3**)
As we think of the gifts we feel seasoned to share.
Let the world see and remember the reason it's there. (**Deuteronomy 15:14, 33:13**)
When we present our gifts with the bet we can offer.
May we give them the gifts that will live on ever after.? **(Romans 4:16, 5:15 to 17, Luke 6:38, Matthew 25:35 and 36)**
The time is coming are you ready to give?
Unto us a child was given so the world might live. (**2nd Corinthians 9:15**)
Let us remember most of all before the season comes to an end.
The greatest giver and the impact delivered brings gifts that never end.
(Acts 2:38, Numbers 18:26-29)
In sincerest thanks to the giver of the greatest gift of life.

GIFTS FROM GOD FOR YOU

I listen for your voice and also hear your request.
So find peace when fear abounds and know I offer rest. (**2nd Chronicles 7:10**)
There is restoration and victory when you listen to what I say.
And know that I am with you as wickedness and evil come your way. (**Job 22:22, Psalm 5:2, 3**)
Offerings from your heart with praises and joyful song.
Will bring me much more pleasure than a gift from doing wrong. (**Psalm 40:6, 58:2-4**)
Wisdom doesn't come from watching others fall.
It comes from hearing our God who knows us one and all. (**Proverbs**)
Not one word that I have spoken has failed to come to pass.
As you listen to my words, know as my covenant my words will last. (**Isaiah 7:14-16**)
For all who are willing to listen I will make their understanding clear.
If you get your wisdom from hearing my voice, you will have no reason to fear (**Acts 38:41**)
And so it is written, from Genesis to Revelation.
All who are willing to hear should listen to what the spirit has to say. (**Revelation 2:29**)
Let me close by saying this:

Psalm 46:10 and 11 "Be silent, and know that I am God. I will be honored by every nation. I will be honored throughout the world."
The Lord almighty is here among us.
The God of Israel is our fortress, amen.
With Love from Your Heavenly Father.

THANKSGIVING WISH FOR YOU

As you are faced with a new season that starts in thankfulness.
Is your heart filled with thing that make you feel blessed?
When you look back on the year and where you have been.
Do You see your future with a hope and joy from within?
If you were asked to share what you are thankful for.
Would the answer make you think for a minute or more?
If the answer isn't clear to the questions given above.
I ask that you receive this with the blessing of love.
Out of all things to be thankful for.
There is only one that spans shore to shore.
It's far more precious than what gold is worth.
It's in the Basic Instructions Before Leaving Earth (**BIBLE**)
The answer is easy when you discover **Psalm 23**.
And it only takes the faith of a tiny mustard seed.
That's just a start if you open your heart and let the light come in.
When you light up your life with **Romans 5:17** your life will never dim.
If you feel there is nothing to hold onto in life.
Ephesians 4:7 and 8 give strength to win your fight.
The greatest reward of Thanksgiving is that of boundless joy.
My biggest wish for you today is that **John 3:16** you enjoy.

AN EASTER TO REMEMBER

Time is drawing near to the return of My Holy Son.
Will **Ephesians 1:5** be the praise coming from your tongue?
The believers who know me will rejoice in that day.
Is **Ephesians 2:6** the promise you hold in your heart today?
My promise is true as eternal life will never end.
Will the word of **Ephesians 3:6** turn a foe into a friend?
My grace and kindness are worthy of highest praise and cheer.
As your heart is humbled in **Romans 3:24** showing my love so dear.
As I have stood by my word in the beginning, you can know my salvation is true.
What I have done for those who believe I will do for Pagans, Mormons and Jews.
What I offer today did not come cheap as my son's blood redeemed you.
But the promise I hold will never grow old in the word of **1st Corinthians 1:2**.
So during this season as memories are reminisced.
Will you see in **2nd Timothy 2:10** why this time still exists?
I have created and rejoice in you for such a time as this.
Let the cheer of **Ephesians 2:10** be the cheer that comes from your lips.
There is a truth I have given you to celebrate every day.
May the words of **Romans 8:2** be the light that shines your way.

Before the sun goes down and you finally kneel to pray.
Will you remember to thank Jesus for giving this special day?
In Reverent Love. Amen.

AGAPE! A VALENTINE FROM GOD

I am the one who created the love that formed you from this earth.
Filled with love unconditional no sin could ever reverse. (**Romans 8:38**)
I have the perfect love alone for such imperfect hearts.
For me I ask you trust in me for I loved you from the start. (**John 4:10**)
I gave you my only precious son, what more could I do?
When I look at the sacrifice I made I see only the good in you. (**Romans 6:23**)
My gifts may go unnoticed but no less valuable that those you see.
I just hope I have made an example that you may share with others in need. (**1st John 4:7**)
I have given much more love that you can even conceive.
If can give you even greater joy if you can others believe. (**John 15:9-11, 2:17 and 18**)
As you wish others love this day in this year of my son.
Remember His beloved sheep before the day is done. (**John 18**)

THE GIFT OF RESURRECTION

There is a special story from **Exodus 12** and **John 14** that rings of bitter joy.
A spotless lamb whose blood was shed that sin could not destroy.
Matthew 26 shares the secret of the price that would have to be paid.
For the only way to freedom was through forgiveness as Jesus prayed.
The sacrifice of the first lamb was eaten and sprinkled on the door.
The final offering of **John 19:30** is the one that lasts forever more.
God loved the world so much that He gave us **John 3:16**.
He even gave His Sinless Son to die for the sinners to be set free.
The bitterness was over when the stone was rolled away.
All that remains is an empty tomb and a promise for us today.
The sadness is for the sinner who has chosen not to believe.
But greater joy is **John 16:23** for those who choose to receive.
Let all who hear these words in light of resurrection day.
Receive the gift of **John 14** in their hearts as they humbly pray.
In the Name of the Perfect Lamb, Amen.

TREASURES OF FELLOWSHIP

Faith is always a work in progress as broken vessels mend
As **Romans 15:1-4** encourage us to follow the masters hand
Eternal Life is a promise as we know in our walk with our Lord
Our peace come in using **1 John 2:25** as our battles victory sword
Love is the key that unlocks the door to our true and humble hearts
When we apply **1 John 3:18** in our lives Gods grace will never depart
Life has much more meaning when reaching out to meet a need
Letting **Ephesians 4 1-6** be the catalyst that starts the growing seed
Obedience in fellowship with God brings forth strength and faith
Finding the path in **Colossians 2:6 and 7** will guide you every day
Worship brings forth miracles in the lives of those you uphold
Seeking joy from **Acts 2:46 and 47** will lead to blessings untold
Sharing the cup that satisfies the body, heart and soul of another
Activates faith of **Hebrews 13:16** that will be remembered forever
Hope for the hopeless and light in the darkness is truly found
As evidence of **1st John 1:5-7** in the lives of believers abound
Intercession is better than any gift this world can possibly offer
Faithfully the words of **Philippians 2:1-2** can heal the wounds of war
Prayer is the secret that holds fast all these treasures of fellowship
Acts 2:42 is the foundation that starts the blessings of friendship

CHAPTER 8

TREASURES FOUND

The section is the bonus section of the book. I have given all the scriptures that inspired and or are included in my writings. My writings would just be nice poems if I did not include the living Word of God in them. The scriptures I have included in my writings make them come alive and make them applicable to your every day life. I have not included all the scriptures because if I did this book would be too big for you to carry around and I want to encourage you to find a Bible and read scriptures not included in my writings. The scriptures I used are just a fraction of the message God wants to share with you. I just wanted to give you a sample so you could taste and see that the Lord is good. The writings included in this book are also a great opportunity for bible studies. There is a lot to be learned but if you go one writing at a time you can learn some delicious ways to enhance your life and be blessed as Jim and I have been blessed. Now it is time to enjoy the treasure you have found.

HIDDEN TREASURES

Psalm 23:1 The Lord is my shepherd; I have everything I need. 2 He lets me rest in green meadows; he leads me beside peaceful streams. 3 He renews my strength. He guides me along right paths, bringing honor to his name. 4 Even when I walk through the dark valley of death, I will not be afraid, for you are close beside me.

Your rod and your staff protect and comfort me. 5 You prepare a feast for me in the presence of my enemies. You welcome me as a guest, anointing my head with oil. My cup overflows with blessings. 6 Surely your goodness and unfailing love will pursue me all the days of my life, and I will live in the house of the Lord forever.

John 3:16 "For God so loved the world that he gave his only Son, so that everyone who believes in him will not perish but have eternal life"

John 14:15 "If you love me, obey my commandments. 16 And I will ask the Father, and he will give you another Counselor, who will never leave you. 17 He is the Holy Spirit, who leads into all truth. The world at large cannot receive him, because it isn't looking for him and doesn't recognize him. But you do, because he lives with you now and later will be in you.

Matthew 5:3 "God blesses those who realize their need for him, for the Kingdom of Heaven is given to them.
 4 God blesses those who mourn, for they will be comforted.
 5 God blesses those who are gentle and lowly, for the whole earth will belong to them.
 6 God blesses those who are hungry and thirsty for justice, for they will receive it in full.
 7 God blesses those who are merciful, for they will be shown mercy.
 8 God blesses those whose hearts are pure, for they will see God.
 9 God blesses those who work for peace, for they will be called the children of God.
 10 God blesses those who are persecuted because they live for God, for the Kingdom of Heaven is theirs.
 11 "God blesses you when you are mocked and persecuted and lied about because you are my followers. 12 Be happy about it! Be very glad! For a great reward awaits you in heaven. And remember, the ancient prophets were persecuted, too.

Matthew 6:9 Pray like this: Our Father in heaven, may your name be honored. 10 May your Kingdom come soon. May your will be done here on earth, just as it is in heaven. 11 Give us our food for today, 12 and forgive us our sins, just as we have forgiven those who have sinned against us. 13 And don't let us yield to temptation, but deliver us from the evil one.

Matthew 6:19 "Don't store up treasures here on earth, where they can be eaten by moths and get rusty, and where thieves break in and steal. 20 Store your treasures in heaven, where they will never become moth-eaten or rusty and where they will be safe from thieves. 21 Wherever your treasure is, there your heart and thoughts will also be.

Matthew 13:44 "The Kingdom of Heaven is like a treasure that a man discovered hidden in a field. In his excitement, he hid it again and sold everything he owned to get enough money to buy the field—and to get the treasure, too! 45 "Again, the Kingdom of Heaven is like a pearl merchant on the lookout for choice pearls. 46 When he discovered a pearl of great value, he sold everything he owned and bought it!

GODS GIVEN TREASURES

Job 28:28 And this is what he says to all humanity: 'the fear of the Lord is true wisdom; to forsake evil is real understanding.'"

Isaiah 2:11 The day is coming when your pride will be brought low and the Lord alone will be exalted.

Isaiah 10: 27 In that day the Lord will end the bondage of his people. He will break the yoke of slavery and lift it from their shoulders.

Isaiah 45:8 Open up, O heavens, and pour out your righteousness. Let the earth open wide so salvation and righteousness can sprout up together. I, the Lord, created them.

Romans 8:17 And since we are his children, we will share his treasures—for everything God gives to his Son, Christ, is ours, too. But if we are to share his glory, we must also share his suffering.

Ephesians 3: 8 Just think! Though I did nothing to deserve it, and though I am the least deserving Christian there is, I was chosen for this special joy of telling the Gentiles about the endless treasures available to them in Christ.

TREASURES OF TRUTH

Isaiah 64:8 And yet, Lord, you are our Father. We are the clay, and you are the potter. We are all formed by your hand.

Hebrews 12:24 You have come to Jesus, the one who mediates the new covenant between God and people, and to the sprinkled blood, which graciously forgives instead of crying out for vengeance as the blood of Abel did.

Revelation 22:11 Let the one who is doing wrong continue to do wrong; the one who is vile, continue to be vile; the one who is good, continue to do good; and the one who is holy, continue in holiness."

Luke 22:19 Then he took a loaf of bread; and when he had thanked God for it, he broke it in pieces and gave it to the disciples, saying, "This is my body, given for you. Do this in remembrance of me."

Romans 8: 11 The Spirit of God, who raised Jesus from the dead, lives in you. And just as he raised Christ from the dead, he will give life to your mortal body by this same Spirit living within you.

Ephesians 1:13 And now you also have heard the truth, the Good News that God saves you. And when you believed in Christ, he identified you as his own by giving you the Holy Spirit, whom he promised long ago.

2nd Corinthians 6:7 We have faithfully preached the truth. God's power has been working in us. We have righteousness as our weapon, both to attack and to defend ourselves.

Ephesians 6:14 Stand your ground, putting on the sturdy belt of truth and the body armor of God's righteousness.

Exodus 19:5 Now if you will obey me and keep my covenant, you will be my own special treasure from among all the nations of the earth; for all the earth belongs to me.

2nd Corinthians 3:14 But the people's minds were hardened, and even to this day whenever the old covenant is being read, a veil covers their minds so they cannot understand the truth. And this veil can be removed only by believing in Christ.

Matthew 5:17 "Don't misunderstand why I have come. I did not come to abolish the law of Moses or the writings of the prophets. No, I came to fulfill them.

Ephesians 6:15 For shoes, put on the peace that comes from the Good News, so that you will be fully prepared.

Hebrews 6:18 So God has given us both his promise and his oath. These two things are unchangeable because it is impossible for God to lie. Therefore, we who have fled to him for refuge can take new courage, for we can hold on to his promise with confidence.

Ephesians 6:16 In every battle you will need faith as your shield to stop the fiery arrows aimed at you by Satan.

TO SEEK AND FIND PENUEL

Jeremiah 23:24 Can anyone hide from me? Am I not everywhere in all the heavens and earth?" asks the Lord.

James 5:16 Confess your sins to each other and pray for each other so that you may be healed. The earnest prayer of a righteous person has great power and wonderful results.

Psalm 133: 1 How wonderful it is, how pleasant, when brothers live together in harmony! 2 For harmony is as precious as the fragrant anointing oil that was poured over Aaron's head, that ran down his beard and onto the border of his robe. 3 Harmony is as refreshing as the dew from Mount Hermon that falls on the mountains of Zion. And the Lord has pronounced his blessing, even life forevermore.

1 John 5:14 And we can be confident that he will listen to us whenever we ask him for anything in line with his will.

John 14:27 "I am leaving you with a gift—peace of mind and heart. And the peace I give isn't like the peace the world gives. So don't be troubled or afraid.

Philippians 1:25 I am convinced of this, so I will continue with you so that you will grow and experience the joy of your faith.

Jeremiah 29:13 If you look for me in earnest, you will find me when you seek me.

TO RECEIVE FROM THE GREATEST GIVING GOD

Matthew 5:6 God blesses those who are hungry and thirsty for justice, for they will receive it in full.

Matthew 10: 41 If you welcome a prophet as one who speaks for God, you will receive the same reward a prophet gets. And if you welcome good and godly people because of their godliness, you will be given a reward like theirs.

Matthew 19:17 "Why ask me about what is good?" Jesus replied. "Only God is good. But to answer your question, you can receive eternal life if you keep the commandments."

Matthew 19:29 And everyone who has given up houses or brothers or sisters or father or mother or children or property, for my sake, will receive a hundred times as much in return and will have eternal life

Matthew 21:22 If you believe, you will receive whatever you ask for in prayer."

Luke 6:36 You must be compassionate, just as your Father is compassionate.

Luke 9:5 If the people of the village won't receive your message when you enter it, shake off its dust from your feet as you leave. It is a sign that you have abandoned that village to its fate."

Luke 10:25 One day an expert in religious law stood up to test Jesus by asking him this question: "Teacher, what must I do to receive eternal life?" 26 Jesus replied, "What does the law of Moses say? How do you read it?" 27 The man answered, "'You must love the Lord your God with all your heart, all your soul, all your strength, and all your mind.' And, 'Love your neighbor as yourself.'" 28 "Right!" Jesus told him. "Do this and you will live!"

John 11:4 But when Jesus heard about it he said, "Lazarus's sickness will not end in death. No, it is for the glory of God. I, the Son of God, will receive glory from this."

John 14:17 He is the Holy Spirit, who leads into all truth. The world at large cannot receive him, because it isn't looking for him and doesn't recognize him. But you do, because he lives with you now and later will be in you.

John 16:21 It will be like a woman experiencing the pains of labor. When her child is born, her anguish gives place to joy because she has brought a new person into the world.

Acts 2:38 Peter replied, "Each of you must turn from your sins and turn to God, and be baptized in the name of Jesus Christ for the forgiveness of your sins. Then you will receive the gift of the Holy Spirit.

Acts 20:35 And I have been a constant example of how you can help the poor by working hard. You should remember the words of the Lord Jesus: 'It is more blessed to give than to receive.'"

VICTORY FOR YOUR SOUL

Isaiah 55:3 "Come to me with your ears wide open. Listen, for the life of your soul is at stake. I am ready to make an everlasting covenant with you. I will give you all the mercies and unfailing love that I promised to David.

Matthew 6: 22 "Your eye is a lamp for your body. A pure eye lets sunshine into your soul.

Matthew 10: 28 "Don't be afraid of those who want to kill you. They can only kill your body; they cannot touch your soul. Fear only God, who can destroy both soul and body in hell.

Matthew 16:26 And how do you benefit if you gain the whole world but lose your own soul in the process? Is anything worth more than your soul?

Matthew 22:37 Jesus replied, "'You must love the Lord your God with all your heart, all your soul, and all your mind.'

3 John 1:2 Dear friend, I am praying that all is well with you and that your body is as healthy as I know your soul is.

Isaiah 30:18 But the Lord still waits for you to come to him so he can show you his love and compassion. For the Lord is a faithful God. Blessed are those who wait for him to help them.

Isaiah 61:8 "For I, the Lord, love justice. I hate robbery and wrongdoing. I will faithfully reward my people for their suffering and make an everlasting covenant with them. 9Their descendants will be known and honored among the nations. Everyone will realize that they are a people the Lord has blessed."

Isaiah 65:23 They will not work in vain, and their children will not be doomed to misfortune. For they are people blessed by the Lord, and their children, too, will be blessed. 24 I will answer them before they even call to me. While they are still talking to me about their needs, I will go ahead and answer their prayers!

Galatians 3:14 Through the work of Christ Jesus, God has blessed the Gentiles with the same blessing he promised to Abraham, and we Christians receive the promised Holy Spirit through faith.

Revelation 14:13 And I heard a voice from heaven saying, "Write this down: Blessed are those who die in the Lord from now on. Yes, says the Spirit, they are blessed indeed, for they will rest from all their toils and trials; for their good deeds follow them!"

Revelation 20:6 Blessed and holy are those who share in the first resurrection. For them the second death holds no power, but they will be priests of God and of Christ and will reign with him a thousand years.

WELCOME THE HOLY SPIRIT INTO YOUR HEART TODAY

John 16: 7 But it is actually best for you that I go away, because if I don't, the Counselor won't come. If I do go away, he will come because I will send him to you.

John 16:.13 When the Spirit of truth comes, he will guide you into all truth. He will not be presenting his own ideas; he will be telling you what he has heard. He will tell you about the future. 14 He will bring me glory by revealing to you whatever he receives from me.

1 Corinthians 12:7 A spiritual gift is given to each of us as a means of helping the entire church.

1 Corinthians 12:8 To one person the Spirit gives the ability to give wise advice; to another he gives the gift of special knowledge. 9 The Spirit gives special faith to another, and to someone else he gives the power to heal the sick. 10 He gives one person the power to perform miracles, and to another the ability to prophesy. He gives someone else the ability to know whether it is really the Spirit of God or another spirit that is speaking. Still another person is given the ability to speak in unknown languages, and another is given the ability to interpret what is being said.

1 Corinthians 12:12 The human body has many parts, but the many parts make up only one body. So it is with the body of Christ.

THE GIFT OF GRACE

Psalm 84:11 For the Lord God is our light and protector. He gives us grace and glory. No good thing will the Lord withhold from those who do what is right.

Joel 2:23 Rejoice, you people of Jerusalem! Rejoice in the Lord your God! For the rains he sends are an expression of his grace. Once more the autumn rains will come, as well as the rains of spring.

Acts 6:8 Stephen, a man full of God's grace and power, performed amazing miracles and signs among the people.

Acts 20:32 "And now I entrust you to God and the word of his grace—his message that is able to build you up and give you an inheritance with all those he has set apart for himself.

Romans 6:14 Sin is no longer your master, for you are no longer subject to the law, which enslaves you to sin. Instead, you are free by God's grace.

1 Corinthians 15:10 But whatever I am now, it is all because God poured out his special favor on me—and not without results. For I have worked harder than all the other apostles, yet it was not I but God who was working through me by his grace.

2 Corinthians 1:12 We can say with confidence and a clear conscience that we have been honest and sincere in all our dealings. We have depended on God's grace, not on our own earthly wisdom. That is how we have acted toward everyone, and especially toward you.

2 Corinthians 4:.15 All of these things are for your benefit. And as God's grace brings more and more people to Christ, there will be great thanksgiving, and God will receive more and more glory.

2 Cornithians 9:14 And they will pray for you with deep affection because of the wonderful grace of God shown through you.

Galatians 2: 21 I am not one of those who treats the grace of God as meaningless. For if we could be saved by keeping the law, then there was no need for Christ to die.

Galatians 5:4 For if you are trying to make yourselves right with God by keeping the law, you have been cut off from Christ! You have fallen away from God's grace.

Titus 2:11 For the grace of God has been revealed, bringing salvation to all people.

Hebrews 2:9 What we do see is Jesus, who "for a little while was made lower than the angels" and now is "crowned with glory and honor" because he suffered death for us. Yes, by God's grace, Jesus tasted death for everyone in all the world.

Hebrews 4:16 So let us come boldly to the throne of our gracious God. There we will receive his mercy, and we will find grace to help us when we need it.

2 John 1:3 May grace, mercy, and peace, which come from God our Father and from Jesus Christ his Son, be with us who live in truth and love.

THE NAME YOU CAN TRUST

Genesis 1:1 In the beginning God created the heavens and the earth. 2 The earth was empty, a formless mass cloaked in darkness. And the Spirit of God was hovering over its surface.

Psalm 19:1 The heavens tell of the glory of God. The skies display his marvelous craftsmanship.

Numbers 23:19 God is not a man, that he should lie. He is not a human, that he should change his mind. Has he ever spoken and failed to act? Has he ever promised and not carried it through?

Exodus 6:2 And God continued, "I am the Lord. 3 I appeared to Abraham, to Isaac, and to Jacob as God Almighty, though I did not reveal my name, the Lord, to them.

Psalm 7:17 I will thank the Lord because he is just; I will sing praise to the name of the Lord Most High.

Genesis 16: 8 The angel said to her, "Hagar, Sarai's servant, where have you come from, and where are you going?" "I am running away from my mistress," she replied.

Psalm 91:1 Those who live in the shelter of the Most High will find rest in the shadow of the Almighty.

Genesis 22:13 Then Abraham looked up and saw a ram caught by its horns in a bush. So he took the ram and sacrificed it as a burnt offering on the altar in place of his son.

Exodus 17:15 Moses built an altar there and called it "The Lord Is My Banner."

Deuteronomy 6:4 "Hear, O Israel! The Lord is our God, the Lord alone.

Psalm 59:5 O Lord God Almighty, the God of Israel, rise up to punish hostile nations. Show no mercy to wicked traitors.

Judges 6:22 When Gideon realized that it was the angel of the Lord, he cried out, "Sovereign Lord, I have seen the angel of the Lord face to face!"

Isaiah 1:4 Oh, what a sinful nation they are! They are loaded down with a burden of guilt. They are evil and corrupt children who have turned away from the Lord. They have despised the Holy One of Israel, cutting themselves off from his help.

Isaiah 6:1 In the year King Uzziah died, I saw the Lord. He was sitting on a lofty throne, and the train of his robe filled the Temple.

Isaiah 40:28 Have you never heard or understood? Don't you know that the Lord is the everlasting God, the Creator of all the earth? He never grows faint or weary. No one can measure the depths of his understanding.

Jeremiah 33:16 In that day Judah will be saved, and Jerusalem will live in safety. And their motto will be 'the Lord is our righteousness!'

Ezekiel 48:35 "The distance around the entire city will be six miles. And from that day the name of the city will be 'the Lord Is There.'"

Daniel 7:13 As my vision continued that night, I saw someone who looked like a man coming with the clouds of heaven. He approached the Ancient One and was led into his presence.

CHARACTERISTICS OF FAVOR WITH GOD

Genesis 6:8 But Noah found favor with the Lord.

Genesis 40:14 And please have some pity on me when you are back in his favor. Mention me to Pharaoh, and ask him to let me out of here.

Nehemiah 1:11 O Lord, please hear my prayer! Listen to the prayers of those of us who delight in honoring you. Please grant me success now as I go to ask the king for a great favor. Put it into his heart to be kind to me." In those days I was the king's cup-bearer.

Nehemiah 13:31 I also made sure that the supply of wood for the altar was brought at the proper times and that the first part of the harvest was collected for the priests. Remember this in my favor, O my God.

Proberbs 3: 34 The Lord mocks at mockers, but he shows favor to the humble.

Proverbs 11:27 If you search for good, you will find favor; but if you search for evil, it will find you!

Proverbs 16:15 When the king smiles, there is life; his favor refreshes like a gentle rain.

Proverbs 18:22 The man who finds a wife finds a treasure and receives favor from the Lord.

Malachi 1:9 "Go ahead, beg God to be merciful to you! But when you bring that kind of offering, why should he show you any favor at all?" asks the Lord Almighty.

Luke 4:19 and that the time of the Lord's favor has come."

Acts 15:11 We believe that we are all saved the same way, by the special favor of the Lord Jesus."

Acts 11:22 When the church at Jerusalem heard what had happened, they sent Barnabas to Antioch.

1 Corinthians 3:10 Because of God's special favor to me, I have laid the foundation like an expert builder. Now others are building on it. But whoever is building on this foundation must be very careful.

1 Corinthians 15:10 But whatever I am now, it is all because God poured out his special favor on me—and not without results. For I have worked harder than all the other apostles, yet it was not I but God who was working through me by his grace.

2 Corinthians 12:9 Each time he said, "My gracious favor is all you need. My power works best in your weakness." So now I am glad to boast about my weaknesses, so that the power of Christ may work through me.

CAN YOU HEAR ME?

Deuteronomy 18:15 "The Lord your God will raise up for you a prophet like me from among your fellow Israelites, and you must listen to that prophet.

Numbers 23:19 God is not a man, that he should lie. He is not a human, that he should change his mind.

Genesis 9:11 I solemnly promise never to send another flood to kill all living creatures and destroy the earth."

Hebrews 12:14 Try to live in peace with everyone, and seek to live a clean and holy life, for those who are not holy will not see the Lord. 15 Look after each other so that none of you will miss out on the special favor of God. Watch out that no bitter root of unbelief rises up among you, for whenever it springs up, many are corrupted by its poison.

Deuteronomy 6:3 Listen closely, Israel, to everything I say. Be careful to obey. Then all will go well with you, and you will have many children in the land flowing with milk and honey, just as the Lord, the God of your ancestors, promised you.

Deuteronomy 7:12 "If you listen to these regulations and obey them faithfully, the Lord your God will keep his covenant of unfailing love with you, as he solemnly promised your ancestors.

2 Chronicles 7:10 Then at the end of the celebration, Solomon sent the people home. They were all joyful and happy because the Lord had been so good to David and Solomon and to his people Israel.

Job 22: 22 Listen to his instructions, and store them in your heart.

Psalm 5:2 Listen to my cry for help, my King and my God, for I will never pray to anyone but you. 3 Listen to my voice in the morning, Lord. Each morning I bring my requests to you and wait expectantly.

Psalm 40:6 You take no delight in sacrifices or offerings. Now that you have made me listen, I finally understand— you don't require burnt offerings or sin offerings.

Psalm 58:2 No, all your dealings are crooked; you hand out violence instead of justice. 3 These wicked people are born sinners; even from birth they have lied and gone their own way. 4 They spit poison like deadly snakes; they are like cobras that refuse to listen

Revelation 2:29 Anyone who is willing to hear should listen to the Spirit and understand what the Spirit is saying to the churches.

IN JESUS NAME

1 Peter 1:3 All honor to the God and Father of our Lord Jesus Christ, for it is by his boundless mercy that God has given us the privilege of being born again. Now we live with a wonderful expectation because Jesus Christ rose again from the dead.

Isaiah 9:6 For a child is born to us, a son is given to us. And the government will rest on his shoulders. These will be his royal titles: Wonderful Counselor, Mighty God, Everlasting Father, Prince of Peace.

John 14:6 Jesus told him, "I am the way, the truth, and the life. No one can come to the Father except through me.

Romans 8:39 Whether we are high above the sky or in the deepest ocean, nothing in all creation will ever be able to separate us from the love of God that is revealed in Christ Jesus our Lord.

John 5:25 "And I assure you that the time is coming, in fact it is here, when the dead will hear my voice—the voice of the Son of God. And those who listen will live.

Hebrews 7:28 Those who were high priests under the law of Moses were limited by human weakness. But after the law was given, God appointed his Son with an oath, and his Son has been made perfect forever.

1 Corinthians 15:45 The Scriptures tell us, "The first man, Adam, became a living person." But the last Adam—that is, Christ—is a life-giving Spirit.

John 6:35 Jesus replied, "I am the bread of life. No one who comes to me will ever be hungry again. Those who believe in me will never thirst.

John 8:12 Jesus said to the people, "I am the light of the world. If you follow me, you won't be stumbling through the darkness, because you will have the light that leads to life."

Revelation 22:13 I am the Alpha and the Omega, the First and the Last, the Beginning and the End."

Revelation 15:1 Then I saw in heaven another significant event, and it was great and marvelous. Seven angels were holding the seven last plagues, which would bring God's wrath to completion.

A FOREVER FATHER

Matthew 5:10 God blesses those who are persecuted because they live for God, for the Kingdom of Heaven is theirs. 11 "God blesses you when you are mocked and persecuted and lied about because you are my followers. 12 Be happy about it! Be very glad! For a great reward awaits you in heaven. And remember, the ancient prophets were persecuted, too.

Mark 14: 36 "Abba, Father," he said, "everything is possible for you. Please take this cup of suffering away from me. Yet I want your will, not mine."

John 15:9 "I have loved you even as the Father has loved me. Remain in my love.

Matthew 19:4 "Haven't you read the Scriptures?" Jesus replied. "They record that from the beginning 'God made them male and female.'

Ephesians 6:1 Children, obey your parents because you belong to the Lord, for this is the right thing to do.

1 Peter 1:3 All honor to the God and Father of our Lord Jesus Christ, for it is by his boundless mercy that God has given us the privilege of being born again. Now we live with a wonderful expectation because Jesus Christ rose again from the dead.

THE LIVING REDEEMER

Leviticus 25:25 If any of your Israelite relatives go bankrupt and are forced to sell some inherited land, then a close relative, a kinsman redeemer, may buy it back for them.

Ruth 3:9 "Who are you?" he demanded. "I am your servant Ruth," she replied. "Spread the corner of your covering over me, for you are my family redeemer." 10 "The Lord bless you, my daughter!"

Boaz exclaimed. "You are showing more family loyalty now than ever by not running after a younger man, whether rich or poor.

Ruth 4:14 And the women of the town said to Naomi, "Praise the Lord who has given you a family redeemer today! May he be famous in Israel.

Job 19:25 "But as for me, I know that my Redeemer lives, and that he will stand upon the earth at last.

Psalm 19:14 May the words of my mouth and the thoughts of my heart be pleasing to you, O Lord, my rock and my redeemer.

Psalm 78:35 Then they remembered that God was their rock, that their redeemer was the Most High.

Isaiah 41:14 Despised though you are, O Israel, don't be afraid, for I will help you. I am the Lord, your Redeemer. I am the Holy One of Israel.'

Isaiah 43:14 The Lord your Redeemer, the Holy One of Israel, says: "For your sakes I will send an invading army against Babylon. And the Babylonians will be forced to flee in those ships they are so proud of.

Isaiah 48:7 "The Lord, your Redeemer, the Holy One of Israel, says: I am the Lord your God, who teaches you what is good and leads you along the paths you should follow.

Isaiah 49:7 The Lord, the Redeemer and Holy One of Israel, says to the one who is despised and rejected by a nation, to the one who is the servant of rulers: "Kings will stand at attention when you pass by. Princes will bow low because the Lord has chosen you. He, the faithful Lord, the Holy One of Israel, chooses you."

Isaiah 54:5 for your Creator will be your husband. The Lord Almighty is his name! He is your Redeemer, the Holy One of Israel, the God of all the earth. 6 For the Lord has called you back from your grief—as though you were a young wife abandoned by her husband," says your God. 7 "For a brief moment I abandoned you, but with great compassion I will take you back. 8 In a moment of anger I turned my face away for a little while. But with everlasting love I will have compassion on you," says the Lord, your Redeemer.

Isaih 60:16 Powerful kings and mighty nations will bring the best of their goods to satisfy your every need. You will know at last that I, the Lord, am your Savior and Redeemer, the Mighty One of Israel.

A SACRIFICE

Psalm 27:6 Then I will hold my head high, above my enemies who surround me.
At his Tabernacle I will offer sacrifices with shouts of joy, singing and praising the Lord with music.

Psalm 40:8 I take joy in doing your will, my God, for your law is written on my heart."

Psalm 50:5 "Bring my faithful people to me— those who made a covenant with me by giving sacrifices."

Psalm 51:17 The sacrifice you want is a broken spirit. A broken and repentant heart, O God, you will not despise.

Psalm 107:22 Let them offer sacrifices of thanksgiving and sing joyfully about his glorious acts.

Psalm 116:18 I will keep my promises to the Lord in the presence of all his people

Psalm 141:2 Accept my prayer as incense offered to you, and my upraised hands as an evening offering.

Proverbs 21:3 The Lord is more pleased when we do what is just and right than when we give him sacrifices.

Matthew 9:13 Then he added, "Now go and learn the meaning of this Scripture: 'I want you to be merciful; I don't want your sacrifices.' For I have come to call sinners, not those who think they are already good enough."

Hebrews 9:26 If that had been necessary, he would have had to die again and again, ever since the world began. But no! He came once for all time, at the end of the age, to remove the power of sin forever by his sacrificial death for us.

Hebrews 10:12 But our High Priest offered himself to God as one sacrifice for sins, good for all time. Then he sat down at the place of highest honor at God's right hand.

Hebrews 10:14 For by that one offering he perfected forever all those whom he is making holy.

1 John 2:2 He is the sacrifice for our sins. He takes away not only our sins but the sins of all the world.

GOD BE WITH YOU

Deuteronomy 31:8 Do not be afraid or discouraged, for the Lord is the one who goes before you. He will be with you; he will neither fail you nor forsake you."

Isaiah 43:2 When you go through deep waters and great trouble, I will be with you. When you go through rivers of difficulty, you will not drown! When you walk through the fire of oppression, you will not be burned up; the flames will not consume you. 3 For I am the Lord, your God, the Holy One of Israel, your Savior. I gave Egypt, Ethiopia, and Seba as a ransom for your freedom.

Philippians 4:9 Keep putting into practice all you learned from me and heard from me and saw me doing, and the God of peace will be with you.

1 Chronicles 22:11 "Now, my son, may the Lord be with you and give you success as you follow his instructions in building the Temple of the Lord your God.

Genesis 28:15 What's more, I will be with you, and I will protect you wherever you go. I will someday bring you safely back to this land. I will be with you constantly until I have finished giving you everything I have promised."

DEAR LORD (PRAYER FOR THE UNBORN)

Leviticus 18:21 "Do not give any of your children as a sacrifice to Molech, for you must not profane the name of your God. I am the Lord.

Psalm 25:12 Who are those who fear the Lord? He will show them the path they should choose. 13 They will live in prosperity, and their children will inherit the Promised Land.

DEAR LORD (A PRAYER OF RESTORATION FOR ALL PEOPLE)

Hebrews 3:15 But never forget the warning: "Today you must listen to his voice.
    Don't harden your hearts against him as Israel did when they rebelled."

1 Peter 4:1 So then, since Christ suffered physical pain, you must arm yourselves with the same attitude he had, and be ready to suffer, too. For if you are willing to suffer for Christ, you have decided to stop sinning.

Romans 5:1 Therefore, since we have been made right in God's sight by faith, we have peace with God because of what Jesus Christ our Lord has done for us. 2 Because of our faith, Christ has brought us into this place of highest privilege where we now stand, and we confidently and joyfully look forward to sharing God's glory.

2 Corinthians 5:20 We are Christ's ambassadors, and God is using us to speak to you. We urge you, as though Christ himself were here pleading with you, "Be reconciled to God!"

2 Corinthians 7:10 For God can use sorrow in our lives to help us turn away from sin and seek salvation. We will never regret that kind of sorrow. But sorrow without repentance is the kind that results in death. 11 Just see what this godly sorrow produced in you! Such earnestness, such concern to clear yourselves, such indignation, such alarm, such longing to see me, such zeal, and such a readiness to punish the wrongdoer. You showed that you have done everything you could to make things right.

Romans 8:28 And we know that God causes everything to work together for the good of those who love God and are called according to his purpose for them. 38 And I am convinced that nothing can ever separate us from his love. Death can't, and life can't. The angels can't, and the demons can't. Our fears for today, our worries about tomorrow, and even the powers of hell can't keep God's love away.

Hebrews 13:5 Stay away from the love of money; be satisfied with what you have. For God has said, "I will never fail you. I will never forsake you." 6 That is why we can say with confidence, "The Lord is my helper, so I will not be afraid. What can mere mortals do to me?"

Luke 15:10 In the same way, there is joy in the presence of God's angels when even one sinner repents."

Luke 19:8 Meanwhile, Zacchaeus stood there and said to the Lord, "I will give half my wealth to the poor, Lord, and if I have overcharged people on their taxes, I will give them back four times as much!" 9 Jesus responded, "Salvation has come to this home today, for this man has shown himself to be a son of Abraham.

Revelation 4:11 "You are worthy, O Lord our God, to receive glory and honor and power. For you created everything, and it is for your pleasure that they exist and were created."

Romans 12:10 Love each other with genuine affection, and take delight in honoring each other.

Mark 12:29 Jesus replied, "The most important commandment is this: 'Hear, O Israel! The Lord our God is the one and only Lord. 30 And you must love the Lord your God with all your heart, all your soul, all your mind, and all your strength.' 31 The second is equally important: 'Love your neighbor as yourself.' No other commandment is greater than these."

Isaiah 40:29 He gives power to those who are tired and worn out; he offers strength to the weak. 30 Even youths will become exhausted, and young men will give up. 31 But those who wait on the Lord will find new strength. They will fly high on wings like eagles. They will run and not grow weary. They will walk and not faint.

Matthew 11:28 Then Jesus said, "Come to me, all of you who are weary and carry heavy burdens, and I will give you rest.

A PRAYER OF BLESSING FOR ALL

John 3:16 "For God so loved the world that he gave his only Son, so that everyone who believes in him will not perish but have eternal life.

Philippians 4:13 For I can do everything with the help of Christ who gives me the strength I need.

Philippians 1:21 For to me, living is for Christ, and dying is even better.

A RIVER OF PRAISE

Romans 15:5 May God, who gives this patience and encouragement, help you live in complete harmony with each other—each with the attitude of Christ Jesus toward the other.

Romans 15:7 So accept each other just as Christ has accepted you; then God will be glorified. 8 Remember that Christ came as a servant to the Jews to show that God is true to the promises he made to their ancestors. 9 And he came so the Gentiles might also give glory to God for his mercies to them. That is what the psalmist meant when he wrote: "I will praise you among the Gentiles; I will sing praises to your name."

1 Corinthians 12:24 while other parts do not require this special care. So God has put the body together in such a way that extra honor and care are given to those parts that have less dignity. 25 This makes for harmony among the members, so that all the members care for each other equally. 26 If one part suffers, all the parts suffer with it, and if one part is honored, all the parts are glad. 27 Now all of you together are Christ's body, and each one of you is a separate and necessary part of it.

Ephesians 2:20 We are his house, built on the foundation of the apostles and the prophets. And the cornerstone is Christ Jesus himself. 21 We who believe are carefully joined together, becoming a holy temple for the Lord. 22 Through him you Gentiles are also joined together as part of this dwelling where God lives by his Spirit.

Ephesians 4:3 Always keep yourselves united in the Holy Spirit, and bind yourselves together with peace.

Philippians 2:2 Then make me truly happy by agreeing wholeheartedly with each other, loving one another, and working together with one heart and purpose.

Colossians 3:14 And the most important piece of clothing you must wear is love. Love is what binds us all together in perfect harmony.

Psalm 133:1 How wonderful it is, how pleasant, when brothers live together in harmony! 2 For harmony is as precious as the fragrant anointing oil that was poured over Aaron's head, that ran down his beard and onto the border of his robe.

Matthew 18:19 "I also tell you this: If two of you agree down here on earth concerning anything you ask, my Father in heaven will do it for you.

Matthew 24:31 And he will send forth his angels with the sound of a mighty trumpet blast, and they will gather together his chosen ones from the farthest ends of the earth and heaven.

Luke 15:6 When you arrived, you would call together your friends and neighbors to rejoice with you because your lost sheep was found.

Acts 10:9 The next day as Cornelius's messengers were nearing the city, Peter went up to the flat roof to pray. It was about noon, 10 and he was hungry. But while lunch was being prepared, he fell into a trance.

THE FINAL REVIVAL

Psalm 119:25 I lie in the dust, completely discouraged; revive me by your word.

Ezekiel 29:21 "And the day will come when I will cause the ancient glory of Israel to revive, and then at last your words will be respected. Then they will know that I am the Lord."

Proverbs 11:25 The generous prosper and are satisfied; those who refresh others will themselves be refreshed.

Isaiah 57:15 The high and lofty one who inhabits eternity, the Holy One, says this: "I live in that high and holy place with those whose spirits are contrite and humble. I refresh the humble and give new courage to those with repentant hearts.

Hebrews 9: 26 If that had been necessary, he would have had to die again and again, ever since the world began. But no! He came once for all time, at the end of the age, to remove the power of sin forever by his sacrificial death for us.

Acts 15:16 'Afterward I will return, and I will restore the fallen kingdom of David.
From the ruins I will rebuild it, and I will restore it,

Psalm 51:10 Create in me a clean heart, O God. Renew a right spirit within me.

Luke 24: 47 With my authority, take this message of repentance to all the nations, beginning in Jerusalem: 'there is forgiveness of sins for all who turn to me.'

Isaiah 40:29 He gives power to those who are tired and worn out; he offers strength to the weak. 30 Even youths will become exhausted, and young men will give up. 31 But those who wait on the Lord will find new strength. They will fly high on wings like eagles. They will run and not grow weary. They will walk and not faint.

WHAT A BLESSING IT IS

Psalm 103:1 Praise the Lord, I tell myself; with my whole heart, I will praise his holy name. 2 Praise the Lord, I tell myself, and never forget the good things he does for me.

Isaiah 65:16 All who invoke a blessing or take an oath will do so by the God of truth. For I will put aside my anger and forget the evil of earlier days.

Hebrews 13:20-21 And now, may the God of peace, who brought again from the dead our Lord Jesus, equip you with all you need for doing his will. May he produce in you, through the power of Jesus Christ, all that is pleasing to him. Jesus is the great Shepherd of the sheep by an everlasting covenant, signed with his blood. To him be glory forever and ever. Amen.

FORGIVENESS

Matthew 6:14 "If you forgive those who sin against you, your heavenly Father will forgive you. 15 But if you refuse to forgive others, your Father will not forgive your sins.

Luke 17:3 I am warning you! If another believer sins, rebuke him; then if he repents, forgive him. 4 Even if he wrongs you seven times a day and each time turns again and asks forgiveness, forgive him."

Matthew 18:21 Then Peter came to him and asked, "Lord, how often should I forgive someone who sins against me? Seven times?" 22 "No!" Jesus replied, "seventy times seven!

Ephesians 4:32 Instead, be kind to each other, tenderhearted, forgiving one another, just as God through Christ has forgiven you.

Mark 2:9 Is it easier to say to the paralyzed man, 'Your sins are forgiven' or 'Get up, pick up your mat, and walk'?

Epheisians 4:2 Be humble and gentle. Be patient with each other, making allowance for each other's faults because of your love. 3 Always keep yourselves united in the Holy Spirit, and bind yourselves together with peace.

Luke 6:37 "Stop judging others, and you will not be judged. Stop criticizing others, or it will all come back on you. If you forgive others, you will be forgiven.

John 20:23 If you forgive anyone's sins, they are forgiven. If you refuse to forgive them, they are unforgiven."

Colossians 3:12 Since God chose you to be the holy people whom he loves, you must clothe yourselves with tenderhearted mercy, kindness, humility, gentleness, and patience. 13 You must make allowance for each other's faults and forgive the person who offends you. Remember, the Lord forgave you, so you must forgive others. 14 And the most important piece of clothing you must wear is love. Love is what binds us all together in perfect harmony.

Mark 11: 25 But when you are praying, first forgive anyone you are holding a grudge against, so that your Father in heaven will forgive your sins, too."

Hebrews 12:14 Try to live in peace with everyone, and seek to live a clean and holy life, for those who are not holy will not see the Lord. 15 Look after each other so that none of you will miss out on the special favor of God. Watch out that no bitter root of unbelief rises up among you, for whenever it springs up, many are corrupted by its poison.

THE HONOR TO LIVE ON

Romans 12:20 Instead, do what the Scriptures say: "If your enemies are hungry, feed them. If they are thirsty, give them something to drink, and they will be ashamed of what they have done to you."

1 Corinthians 12:23 And the parts we regard as less honorable are those we clothe with the greatest care. So we carefully protect from the eyes of others those parts that should not be seen, 26 If one part suffers, all the parts suffer with it, and if one part is honored, all the parts are glad.

2 Corinthians 8:21 We are careful to be honorable before the Lord, but we also want everyone else to know we are honorable.

Philippians 4:8 And now, dear brothers and sisters, let me say one more thing as I close this letter. Fix your thoughts on what is true and honorable and right. Think about things that are pure and lovely and admirable. Think about things that are excellent and worthy of praise. 9 Keep putting into practice all you learned from me and heard from me and saw me doing, and the God of peace will be with you.

1 Peter 2:12 Be careful how you live among your unbelieving neighbors. Even if they accuse you of doing wrong, they will see your honorable behavior, and they will believe and give honor to God when he comes to judge the world.

AN OFFERING IN STONE

1 Peter 2

WHY UNITED WE STAND

Deuteronomy 7: 23 But the Lord your God will hand them over to you. He will throw them into complete confusion until they are destroyed. 24 He will put their kings in your power, and you will erase their names from the face of the earth. No one will be able to stand against you, and you will destroy them all.

Exodus 14:13 But Moses told the people, "Don't be afraid. Just stand where you are and watch the Lord rescue you. The Egyptians that you see today will never be seen again. 14 The Lord himself will fight for you. You won't have to lift a finger in your defense!"

2 Chronicles 20:9 They said, 'Whenever we are faced with any calamity such as war, disease, or famine, we can come to stand in your presence before this Temple where your name is honored. We can cry out to you to save us, and you will hear us and rescue us.'
17 But you will not even need to fight. Take your positions; then stand still and watch the Lord's victory. He is with you, O people of Judah and Jerusalem. Do not be afraid or discouraged. Go out there tomorrow, for the Lord is with you!"

Galatians 5:1 So Christ has really set us free. Now make sure that you stay free, and don't get tied up again in slavery to the law.

2 Samuel 22:33 God is my strong fortress; he has made my way safe. 34 He makes me as surefooted as a deer, leading me safely along the mountain heights. 35 He prepares me for battle; he strengthens me to draw a bow of bronze. 36 You have given me the shield of your salvation; your help has made me great. 37 You have made a wide path for my feet to keep them from slipping.

Matthew 12:25 Jesus knew their thoughts and replied, "Any kingdom at war with itself is doomed. A city or home divided against itself is doomed.

1 Corinthians 15:58 So, my dear brothers and sisters, be strong and steady, always enthusiastic about the Lord's work, for you know that nothing you do for the Lord is ever useless.

Isaiah 14:24 The Lord Almighty has sworn this oath: "It will all happen as I have planned. It will come about according to my purposes. 25 I will break the Assyrians when they are in Israel; I will trample them on my mountains. My people will no longer be their slaves.

Isaiah 7:9 Israel is no stronger than its capital, Samaria. And Samaria is no stronger than its king, Pekah son of Remaliah. You do not believe me? If you want me to protect you, learn to believe what I say."

PEACE FOR FREEDOM

Colossians 1:20 and by him God reconciled everything to himself. He made peace with everything in heaven and on earth by means of his blood on the cross.

Micah 5:4 And he will stand to lead his flock with the Lord's strength, in the majesty of the name of the Lord his God. Then his people will live there undisturbed, for he will be highly honored all around the world. 5 And he will be the source of our peace.

Romans 5:1 Therefore, since we have been made right in God's sight by faith, we have peace with God because of what Jesus Christ our Lord has done for us. 2 Because of our faith, Christ has brought us into this place of highest privilege where we now stand, and we confidently and joyfully look forward to sharing God's glory.

Ephesians 2:13 But now you belong to Christ Jesus. Though you once were far away from God, now you have been brought near to him because of the blood of Christ. 14 For Christ himself has made peace between us Jews and you Gentiles by making us all one people. He has broken down the wall of hostility that used to separate us.

1 Timothy 1:1 This letter is from Paul, an apostle of Christ Jesus, appointed by the command of God our Savior and by Christ Jesus our hope. 2 It is written to Timothy, my true child in the faith. May God our Father and Christ Jesus our Lord give you grace, mercy, and peace.

9/11 VICTORY PRAYER

Ephesians 6:10 A final word: Be strong with the Lord's mighty power. 11 Put on all of God's armor so that you will be able to stand firm against all strategies and tricks of the Devil. 12 For we are not fighting against people made of flesh and blood, but against the evil rulers and authorities of the unseen world, against those mighty powers of darkness who rule this world, and against wicked spirits in the heavenly realms. 13 Use every piece of God's armor to resist the enemy in the time of evil, so that after the battle you will still be standing firm. 14 Stand your ground, putting on the sturdy belt of truth and the body armor of God's righteousness. 15 For shoes, put on the peace that comes from the Good News, so that you will be fully prepared.

BELIEVERS VICTORY SONG

Revelation 1:6 He has made us his kingdom and his priests who serve before God his Father. Give to him everlasting glory! He rules forever and ever! Amen!

1 Peter 5:2 Care for the flock of God entrusted to you. Watch over it willingly, not grudgingly—not for what you will get out of it, but because you are eager to serve God.

1 Timothy 1:12 How thankful I am to Christ Jesus our Lord for considering me trustworthy and appointing me to serve him,

Galatians 5:13 For you have been called to live in freedom—not freedom to satisfy your sinful nature, but freedom to serve one another in love. 14 For the whole law can be summed up in this one command: "Love your neighbor as yourself." 15 But if instead of showing love among yourselves you are always biting and devouring one another, watch out! Beware of destroying one another.

2 Corinthians 6:6 We have proved ourselves by our purity, our understanding, our patience, our kindness, our sincere love, and the power of the Holy Spirit.

1 Corinthians 16:13 Be on guard. Stand true to what you believe. Be courageous. Be strong. 14 And everything you do must be done with love. 15 You know that Stephanas and his household were the first to become Christians in Greece, and they are spending their lives in service to other Christians. I urge you, dear brothers and sisters, 16 to respect them fully and others like them who serve with such real devotion.

Romans 14:17 For the Kingdom of God is not a matter of what we eat or drink, but of living a life of goodness and peace and joy in the Holy Spirit. 18 If you serve Christ with this attitude, you will please God. And other people will approve of you, too. 19 So then, let us aim for harmony in the church and try to build each other up.

WELCOME TO A PLACE CALLED HEAVEN

Isaiah 57:15 The high and lofty one who inhabits eternity, the Holy One, says this: "I live in that high and holy place with those whose spirits are contrite and humble. I refresh the humble and give new courage to those with repentant hearts.

James 4:10 When you bow down before the Lord and admit your dependence on him, he will lift you up and give you honor.

Matthew 5:3 "God blesses those who realize their need for him, for the Kingdom of Heaven is given to them.

Matthew 11:11 "I assure you, of all who have ever lived, none is greater than John the Baptist. Yet even the most insignificant person in the Kingdom of Heaven is greater than he is!

Revelation 22:15 Outside the city are the dogs—the sorcerers, the sexually immoral, the murderers, the idol worshipers, and all who love to live a lie.

James 2:5 Listen to me, dear brothers and sisters. Hasn't God chosen the poor in this world to be rich in faith? Aren't they the ones who will inherit the kingdom God promised to those who love him?

Matthew 13:41 I, the Son of Man, will send my angels, and they will remove from my Kingdom everything that causes sin and all who do evil. 33 Jesus also used this illustration: "The Kingdom of Heaven is like yeast used by a woman making bread. Even though she used a large amount of flour, the yeast permeated every part of the dough."

Matthew 18: 4 Therefore, anyone who becomes as humble as this little child is the greatest in the Kingdom of Heaven.

Matthew 16:19 And I will give you the keys of the Kingdom of

Heaven. Whatever you lock on earth will be locked in heaven, and whatever you open on earth will be opened in heaven."

A MESSAGE OF HOPE AND UNDERSTANDING

2 Timothy 2:11 This is a true saying: If we die with him, we will also live with him. 12 If we endure hardship, we will reign with him. If we deny him, he will deny us. 13 If we are unfaithful, he remains faithful, for he cannot deny himself.

THE GIFT OF TIME

Ecclesiastes 3: 1 There is a time for everything, a season for every activity under heaven.
    2 A time to be born and a time to die. A time to plant and a time to harvest.
    3 A time to kill and a time to heal. A time to tear down and a time to rebuild.
    4 A time to cry and a time to laugh. A time to grieve and a time to dance.
    5 A time to scatter stones and a time to gather stones. A time to embrace and a time to turn away.
    6 A time to search and a time to lose. A time to keep and a time to throw away.
    7 A time to tear and a time to mend. A time to be quiet and a time to speak up.
    8 A time to love and a time to hate. A time for war and a time for peace.

YEAR OF DEDICATION AND DECLARATION

Matthew 5: 15 Don't hide your light under a basket! Instead, put it on a stand and let it shine for all.

2 Timothy 2:7 For God has not given us a spirit of fear and timidity, but of power, love, and self-discipline.

Luke 11:35 Make sure that the light you think you have is not really darkness. 36 If you are filled with light, with no dark corners, then your whole life will be radiant, as though a floodlight is shining on you."

1 John 1:7 But if we are living in the light of God's presence, just as Christ is, then we have fellowship with each other, and the blood of Jesus, his Son, cleanses us from every sin.

Isaiah 58:6 "No, the kind of fasting I want calls you to free those who are wrongly imprisoned and to stop oppressing those who work for you. Treat them fairly and give them what they earn. 7 I want you to share your food with the hungry and to welcome poor wanderers into your homes. Give clothes to those who need them, and do not hide from relatives who need your help.

James 1:12 God blesses the people who patiently endure testing. Afterward they will receive the crown of life that God has promised to those who love him.

Matthew 4:16 the people who sat in darkness have seen a great light. And for those who lived in the land where death casts its shadow, a light has shined."

Matthew 5:16 In the same way, let your good deeds shine out for all to see, so that everyone will praise your heavenly Father.

Isaiah 8:20 "Check their predictions against my testimony," says the Lord. "If their predictions are different from mine, it is because there is no light or truth in them.

Luke 19:17 'Well done!' the king exclaimed. 'You are a trustworthy servant. You have been faithful with the little I entrusted to you, so you will be governor of ten cities as your reward.'

LET GLORY REIGN ON THE YEAR OF YOUR HOLY ONE

Ephesians 6:23 May God give you peace, dear brothers and sisters, and love with faith, from God the Father and the Lord Jesus Christ.

Hebrews 8:6 But our High Priest has been given a ministry that is far superior to the ministry of those who serve under the old laws, for he is the one who guarantees for us a better covenant with God, based on better promises.

Ephesians 1:13 And now you also have heard the truth, the Good News that God saves you. And when you believed in Christ, he identified you as his own by giving you the Holy Spirit, whom he promised long ago.

Matthew 6:33 and he will give you all you need from day to day if you live for him and make the Kingdom of God your primary concern.

Galatians 6:9 So don't get tired of doing what is good. Don't get discouraged and give up, for we will reap a harvest of blessing at the appropriate time.

Deuteronomy 2:7 The Lord your God has blessed everything you have done and has watched your every step through this great wilderness. During these forty years, the Lord your God has been with you and provided for your every need so that you lacked nothing.'"

Psalm 37:5 Commit everything you do to the Lord, Trust him, and he will help you.

Ecclesiastes 9:9 Live happily with the woman you love through all the meaningless days of life that God has given you in this world. The wife God gives you is your reward for all your earthly toil.

1 Corinthians 1:4 I can never stop thanking God for all the generous gifts he has given you, now that you belong to Christ Jesus.

Psalm 84:11 For the Lord God is our light and protector. He gives us grace and glory. No good thing will the Lord withhold from those who do what is right.

THE YEAR OF SPIRITUAL EYES TO SEE

1 Timothy 3:16 Without question, this is the great mystery of our faith: Christ appeared in the flesh and was shown to be righteous by the Spirit. He was seen by angels and was announced to the nations. He was believed on in the world and was taken up into heaven.

Ecclesiastes 7:2 It is better to spend your time at funerals than at festivals. For you are going to die, and you should think about it while there is still time.

Romans 8:29 For God knew his people in advance, and he chose them to become like his Son, so that his Son would be the firstborn, with many brothers and sisters. 30 And having chosen them, he called them to come to him. And he gave them right standing with himself, and he promised them his glory.

1 John 3:2 Yes, dear friends, we are already God's children, and we can't even imagine what we will be like when Christ returns. But we do know that when he comes we will be like him, for we will see him as he really is. 3 And all who believe this will keep themselves pure, just as Christ is pure.

Psalm 73:17 Then one day I went into your sanctuary, O God, and I thought about the destiny of the wicked.

THE PERFECT GIFT FOR CHRISTMAS

Acts 3:5 The lame man looked at them eagerly, expecting a gift. 6 But Peter said, "I don't have any money for you. But I'll give you what I have. In the name of Jesus Christ of Nazareth, get up and walk!"

Romans 4:4 When people work, their wages are not a gift. Workers earn what they receive.

John 14:27 "I am leaving you with a gift—peace of mind and heart. And the peace I give isn't like the peace the world gives. So don't be troubled or afraid.

Ephesians 2:8 God saved you by his special favor when you believed. And you can't take credit for this; it is a gift from God.

John 4:10 Jesus replied, "If you only knew the gift God has for you and who I am, you would ask me, and I would give you living water."

1 Chronicles 16:3 Then he gave a gift of food to every man and woman in Israel: a loaf of bread, a cake of dates, and a cake of raisins.

Matthew 6:2 When you give a gift to someone in need, don't shout about it as the hypocrites do—blowing trumpets in the synagogues and streets to call attention to their acts of charity! I assure you, they have received all the reward they will ever get.

Romans 12:7 If your gift is that of serving others, serve them well. If you are a teacher, do a good job of teaching. 8 If your gift is to encourage others, do it! If you have money, share it generously. If God has given you leadership ability, take the responsibility seriously. And if you have a gift for showing kindness to others, do it gladly.

1 Peter 4:10 God has given gifts to each of you from his great variety of spiritual gifts. Manage them well so that God's generosity can flow through you.

Epheisans 5:16 Make the most of every opportunity for doing good in these evil days.

Proverbs 25:14 A person who doesn't give a promised gift is like clouds and wind that don't bring rain.

Leviticus 7:29 "Give these further instructions to the Israelites: When you present a peace offering to the Lord, bring part of it as a special gift to the Lord.

Matthew 23:19 How blind! For which is greater, the gift on the altar, or the altar that makes the gift sacred? 20 When you swear 'by the altar,' you are swearing by it and by everything on it. 21 And when you swear 'by the Temple,' you are swearing by it and by God, who lives in it.

Luke 6:38 If you give, you will receive. Your gift will return to you in full measure, pressed down, shaken together to make room for more, and running over. Whatever measure you use in giving—large or small—it will be used to measure what is given back to you."

Psalm 127:3 Children are a gift from the Lord; they are a reward from him.

Deuteronomy 15:14 Give him a generous farewell gift from your flock, your threshing floor, and your winepress. Share with him some of the bounty with which the Lord your God has blessed you.

Deuteronomy 33:13 Moses said this about the tribes of Joseph: "May their land be blessed by the Lord with the choice gift of rain from the heavens, and water from beneath the earth;

Romans 4:16 So that's why faith is the key! God's promise is given to us as a free gift. And we are certain to receive it, whether or not we follow Jewish customs, if we have faith like Abraham's. For Abraham is the father of all who believe.

Matthew 25:35 For I was hungry, and you fed me. I was thirsty, and you gave me a drink. I was a stranger, and you invited me into your home. 36 I was naked, and you gave me clothing. I was sick, and you cared for me. I was in prison, and you visited me.'

2 Corinthians 9:15 Thank God for his Son—a gift too wonderful for words!

Acts 2:38 Peter replied, "Each of you must turn from your sins and turn to God, and be baptized in the name of Jesus Christ for the forgiveness of your sins. Then you will receive the gift of the Holy Spirit.

GIFTS FROM GOD FOR YOU

2 Chronicles 7:10 Then at the end of the celebration, Solomon sent the people home. They were all joyful and happy because the Lord had been so good to David and Solomon and to his people Israel.

Job 22:22 Listen to his instructions, and store them in your heart.

Psalm 5:2 Listen to my cry for help, my King and my God, for I will never pray to anyone but you. 3 Listen to my voice in the morning, Lord. Each morning I bring my requests to you and wait expectantly.

Psalm 40:6 You take no delight in sacrifices or offerings. Now that you have made me listen, I finally understand— you don't require burnt offerings or sin offerings.

Revelation 2:29 Anyone who is willing to hear should listen to the Spirit and understand what the Spirit is saying to the churches.

THANKSGIVING WISH FOR YOU

Romans 5:17 The sin of this one man, Adam, caused death to rule over us, but all who receive God's wonderful, gracious gift of righteousness will live in triumph over sin and death through this one man, Jesus Christ.

Ephesians 4:7 However, he has given each one of us a special gift according to the generosity of Christ. 8 That is why the Scriptures say, "When he ascended to the heights, he led a crowd of captives and gave gifts to his people."

AN EASTER TO REMEMBER

Epheisans 1:5 His unchanging plan has always been to adopt us into his own family by bringing us to himself through Jesus Christ. And this gave him great pleasure.

Ephesians 2:6 For he raised us from the dead along with Christ, and we are seated with him in the heavenly realms—all because we are one with Christ Jesus.

Ephesians 3:6 And this is the secret plan: The Gentiles have an equal share with the Jews in all the riches inherited by God's children. Both groups have believed the Good News, and both are part of the same body and enjoy together the promise of blessings through Christ Jesus.

Romans 3:24 Yet now God in his gracious kindness declares us not guilty. He has done this through Christ Jesus, who has freed us by taking away our sins.

1 Corinthians 1:2 We are writing to the church of God in Corinth, you who have been called by God to be his own holy people. He made you holy by means of Christ Jesus, just as he did all Christians everywhere—whoever calls upon the name of Jesus Christ, our Lord and theirs.

2 Timothy 2:10 I am willing to endure anything if it will bring salvation and eternal glory in Christ Jesus to those God has chosen.

Ephesians 2:10 For we are God's masterpiece. He has created us anew in Christ Jesus, so that we can do the good things he planned for us long ago.

Romans 8:2 For the power of the life-giving Spirit has freed you through Christ Jesus from the power of sin that leads to death.

AGAPE! A VALENTINE FROM GOD

Romans 8:38 And I am convinced that nothing can ever separate us from his love. Death can't, and life can't. The angels can't, and the demons can't. Our fears for today, our worries about tomorrow, and even the powers of hell can't keep God's love away.

John 4:10 Jesus replied, "If you only knew the gift God has for you and who I am, you would ask me, and I would give you living water."

Romans 6:23 For the wages of sin is death, but the free gift of God is eternal life through Christ Jesus our Lord.

1 John 4:7 Dear friends, let us continue to love one another, for love comes from God. Anyone who loves is born of God and knows God. 8 But anyone who does not love does not know God—for God is love.

THE GIFT OF RESURRECTION

John 19: 30 When Jesus had tasted it, he said, "It is finished!" Then he bowed his head and gave up his spirit.

John 16:23 At that time you won't need to ask me for anything. The truth is, you can go directly to the Father and ask him, and he will grant your request because you use my name.

TREASURES OF FELLOWSHIP

1 John 2:25 And in this fellowship we enjoy the eternal life he promised us.

John 3:18 "There is no judgment awaiting those who trust him. But those who do not trust him have already been judged for not believing in the only Son of God.

Hebrews 13:16 Don't forget to do good and to share what you have with those in need, for such sacrifices are very pleasing to God.

Acts 2:42 They joined with the other believers and devoted themselves to the apostles' teaching and fellowship, sharing in the Lord's Supper and in prayer.

Printed in the United States
26608LVS00007B/79-306